Science Fair Projects

An Inquiry-Based Guide

by Pamela J. Galus

Cover design by Matthew Van Zomeren
Inside illustrations by Janet Armbrust

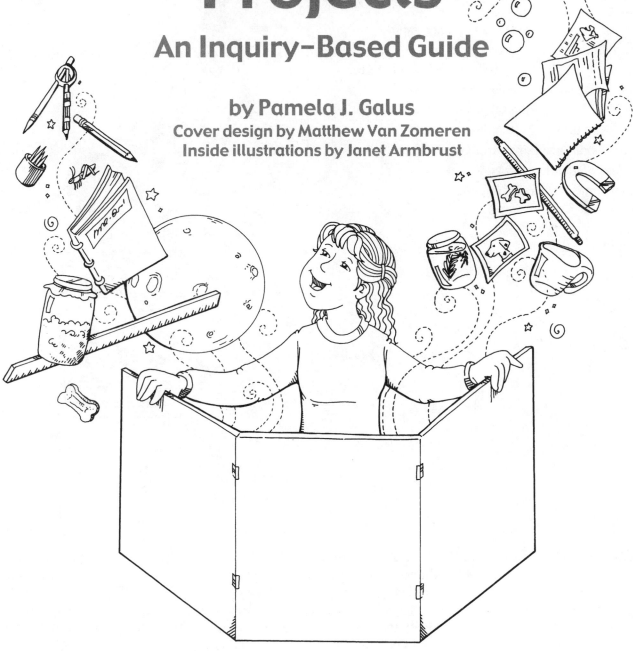

Carson-Dellosa Publishing Company, Inc.
Greensboro, North Carolina

Dedication

In memory of Dan Galus, my partner in life, an incredible man who supported me in every way

To Rita (DarDar) Pedersen, an amazing person whose love and caring touches so many lives—I'm glad she is part of my world

Credits

Author: Pamela J. Galus

Cover art direction: Annette Hollister-Papp

Cover design: Matthew Van Zomeren

Cover photographs: © Comstock, Inc., © Photodisc, and © Digital Stock Corporation

Editors: Kelly Gunzenhauser, Debra Olson Pressnall, Karen Seberg

Inside illustrations: Janet Armbrust

Page design/graphics: Jon Nawrocik

Page layout: River Road Graphics

Printed in the USA   ISBN 0-88724-949-3

TABLE OF CONTENTS

INTRODUCTION

Science fairs and science classes are the times when you know you are thinking about and doing science. However, when you get right down to it, you've been doing science your whole life. Have you ever been shocked by electricity? Perhaps when you were very young, you watched your mom change a lightbulb, and thought it was interesting that the bulb lit up in the socket and not in her hand. Without even realizing it, you may have thought of a hypothesis and a way to conduct the experiment. (Did you stick your finger in the socket? Ouch!) Or, maybe you just scraped your shoes across the carpet a few times and then touched your little brother to make him squeal when the excess electrons jumped from your hand to his body. To do that, you had to figure out that scraping your shoes across the carpet might be a way to shock people—then you had to test your hypothesis. See, you're an expert at science experiments already!

Why do we have to do science fair projects?

You might think that you are doing a science fair project just because it's required or so you can get extra credit, but there is much more to it. The science you do in science class usually involves doing what someone else tells you to do. Science fairs let you actually do science on your own: you pick a topic that sounds interesting, you decide how you want to study it, and you decide how hard your project will be and how much time you want to spend on it! As you study your topic, you will experience science in a whole new way. The experience you gain through your science fair project may solve problems in the future or enrich people's lives. So, the main purpose of a science fair is for you to ask your own question and search for your own solution!

There is also another reason teachers encourage students to participate in science fairs. You have probably learned about something called the "process of science" or the "scientific method" in school. Usually, these terms refer to the way scientists organize information. In the real world, there are many ways to study a problem, but scientists prefer to use this particular method—the same method you need to use when you conduct your investigation. When your project is finished, judges will be looking for evidence that you can use an organized approach to solve problems or study a topic.

How to use this book

This book will help you do several things. First, it will teach you how to choose a good topic and then research it. Next, it will explain you the parts of a good experiment. It will also teach you how to create an experiment and will even give you some sample experiments that will help you think of your own! Finally, this book will help you be prepared for the judging of your project.

How much help can I get?

One thing is for sure—you will need help with your project from time to time and you should not hesitate to ask! Collaboration is the spirit and the strength of science. Scientists work together and share information all the time. Think of any person with more experience as a "guide on the side." It is fine for others to offer advice on any aspect of your project and help you figure out how to obtain specific equipment and how to use it safely. Adults have more experience and their suggestions might prevent you from hurting yourself or someone else.

The problem is that if someone helps too much, it really is not your project. Remember, judges will be asking you questions about your project, and they will know if you have had so much help that your project became someone else's work. You will always want to attempt to find your own solution to any problems you have. Once you have done the work and think you have the answer, then ask an adult if she/he think your solution will work. You might be surprised at how good you are at solving your own problems.

OK	Probably NOT OK (ask your teacher)
Ask your science teacher to approve your idea.	Copy idea straight from your science book.
Have an adult help you find supplies to purchase.	Send someone out to buy supplies for you.
Ask an adult how to use safety equipment.	Have an adult do the experiment.
Get someone to proofread your report.	Ask someone to write your report.
Ask for help on your bibliography.	Have someone else do the research for you.
Show a sketch of your graphs to an adult.	Have an adult create the graphs for you.
Try to decide why the experiment did not go as planned.	Ask an adult what went wrong.
Get help making nice graphics for your display.	Have someone make the display for you.

How will I ever get finished in time?

As long as you start far enough ahead of schedule (at least five weeks or longer if your experiment is long), you should have no trouble finishing in plenty of time. If you think of all the things you need to do at one time, you will be overwhelmed. So, break the project into little chunks, and do a little at a time. Use the worksheets from pages 10–31 to help you think through the process, then use the scheduling checklist (page 7) to schedule your project and check off each item as you finish.

Vocabulary Quick-Reference Chart

Before you can plan anything well, you need to know all of the parts of an experiment. Use this page like you would use a dictionary to help you understand the parts of a science fair experiment. The following terms are also explained more in-depth on pages 7–34.

Conclusion • Your opinion about what happened during the experiment; included at the end of the report

Control group • The group of test subjects that you use to show what happens when the independent variable is not applied

Data • These are also observations, but they are listed in the form of a chart or graph, so that you can clearly see the results from the data.

Dependent variable • The change that happens in your experiment as the result of the independent variable

Display • A backboard, often three-paneled, on which is attached the title of the experiment, parts of the written report, graphs and charts, pictures, etc. to tell the story of your entire experiment

Documentation • Information about each source you used for research that would enable anyone looking at your project to find the sources again

Experimental group • The group of test subjects that you use to show what happens when the independent variable is applied

Formal journal • A notebook (usually a three-ring binder) that you can use to organize the final pieces of your experiment

Hypothesis • A testable statement that you make as an answer to the question you have about your topic; an important statement used to guide the entire experiment

Independent variable • The one thing that you change in your experiment to figure out what impact it has on the topic you study

Informal journal • A journal in which you will write everything, including notes, doodles, brainstorming, questions, problems, etc.

Materials list • A list of all the supplies you use for your experiment

Observations • All of the information you write in your informal journal and summarize in your data as you conduct your experiment

Oral presentation • A talk about your work that you may have with other students, teachers, and judges

Procedure • A list of the steps you complete to perform your experiment from start to finish

Question • What you want to know about your topic that forms the basis for your hypothesis

Report • A typed or neatly written explanation about your project which goes into your formal journal (along with your informal journal)

Research • Any information you gather from different sources (books, the Internet, magazine articles, interviews of specialists, etc.) which helps you know more about your science project topic

Results • A simple, factual summary of what happened in the experiment

Topic • The area of interest in which you will perform your experiment, such as plants, electrical conductors, coins, etc.; anything that is interesting to you that can be used to create an experiment

Variable • Anything that affects your topic and can change in your experiment

HOW THE PARTS COME TOGETHER

Observations

Science begins and ends with observation, and it has observation all the way through the middle. Scientists are trained observers. Even if you do not think of yourself as a scientist, making observations is easy—you do it all the time! Observations are just things you notice with your five senses. You already observe many things, but you may not think that much about what you see, hear, taste, touch, or smell. As you do your experiment, you must train yourself to notice even the slightest change. You will start observing as soon as you begin the process of selecting a topic. Then, you should start recording those observations in a science journal. You will need both an informal journal and a formal journal.

Informal Journal

For your daily observation journal, you will probably want a small spiral-bound notebook in which you can record your thoughts and impressions each day during the experiment. Have it with you whenever you do anything with your project, so that you can write everything you see and do as you go. When you do the brainstorming exercises and worksheets (pages 10–16), keep track of the process in your journal. List where you find supplies and what brands they are. Draw pictures of your experiment setup, and draw what happens to your plants or animals or items. (You can be messy and draw pictures in the spiral-bound notebook, because you will either type or rewrite the information and organize it later.) Make a note of how things appear (color, shape, etc.), what amounts you use of different materials, how long the process takes, and what happens as a result. Wish you had done something differently? Write it down! Be as thorough as you can—no observation is too small or unimportant.

How does the informal journal work with worksheets?

If you choose to use the worksheets in this book, writing all the information over again in your notebook may be a lot of unnecessary work. Check with your teacher before writing on the worksheets. If your teacher allows you to use the worksheets and keep them with your observations, you can place them in your informal journal. (Staple the worksheets to pages or punch holes in them and add them to the formal journal in the same section as your informal journal.) If it is not allowed, use the worksheets as models for what you write in your informal journal.

Formal Journal

For the formal, typewritten version of your observations and report, a three-ring binder can hold a lot of papers and can be divided into many sections and still look tidy. You can use tabbed dividers to help you organize your notebook and move things around as needed. Since you never know what the judges might ask to see at the science fair (they often like to see the "raw thinking" behind your polished, finished lab report and display), it is best to include as much as you can without making your display area look sloppy. You can put the entire informal journal (the spiral notebook) in the binder behind the tab that says "Experimental Notes." The sections can be divided in any way that makes sense to you. You will probably want to have tabs that say: Introduction, Experimental Procedure, Data, Results, Conclusion, Experimental Notes, Research Notes, and References/Acknowledgments.

Topic

The topic is the area of interest in which you will perform your experiment. Examples are plants, electrical conductors, coins, etc. In short, your topic can be anything that is interesting to you that can be used to create an experiment.

Question

Your project will be much better and more fun if you pick a topic that interests you. Remember, you will be working on this project for a very long time. You have spent your whole life learning and observing so there is a science fair project in your head already. You just need to find a way to get it out. Before you start, here are some guidelines. The best science fair ideas come from questions you have about things in your life. Choose a question that will form the basis for your hypothesis. *However, if a question can be answered with "yes" or "no," it is not a good topic.* For example, if your science fair question is, "Does my little sister like broccoli?" The answer is probably "no." To make a good science fair topic, you could ask, "How can broccoli be served so that five-year-old children will eat it?" See the difference? You cannot answer the second question with a yes or no. To find the answer, you would have to find several five-year-old children and try serving them broccoli that has been prepared many different ways.

If you are having difficulty selecting a topic for your science fair project, use the worksheets on pages 10–16 to help you think of ideas that are in your head and write them down. Some ways to find a topic that interests you are given in this section. You can try all the topic searches or just the one that you think will work best for you. We suggest that you try all of the brainstorming activities and come up with several topic ideas before you pick your project topic.

Name _____   **Date** _____

Scheduling the Project

Scheduling the time your experiment will take is important. Plan on finishing your project two weeks before the science fair so that you can practice your presentation several times. Begin by making a list of the things that must be done. Plan the date that you would like to have each item completed.

Complete-by Date	Activity	Actual Date Completed
At least 10 weeks before*	___ Select a topic. ___ Research the topic. ___ State the hypothesis. ___ Plan the procedure. ___ Gather materials.	_____ _____ _____ _____ _____
At least 8 weeks before*	___ Begin the first experiment. ___ Complete the first experiment. ___ Repeat the experiment.	_____ _____ _____
At least 4 weeks before	___ Begin the written report. ___ Complete the research. ___ Graph the data on a computer or paper.	_____ _____ _____
At least 3 weeks before	___ Complete the written report. ___ Locate a display board. ___ Begin creating the display. ___ Finish section 1 of display board. ___ Finish section 2 of display board. ___ Finish section 3 of display board.	_____ _____ _____ _____ _____ _____
At least 2 weeks before	___ Select items from experiment to display. ___ Practice presentation in front of a mirror. ___ Practice presentation with parents. ___ Practice presentation with friends.	_____ _____ _____ _____

* Note that these times may vary, depending on when your school asks you to begin preparing for the science fair and on how long your experiment will take.

Topic Search: Freewriting

Set a timer for five minutes. During those five minutes, write continuously. Write your thoughts on this paper first and then continue writing on blank sheets of notebook paper. Write any thought that comes to your mind, whether it is science related or not. That means that your pen never leaves the paper. The first words you will write should be, "The things that interest me the most are . . ." and then just set your thoughts free. If you cannot think of anything, just keep writing, "The things that interest me the most are . . ." Your brain hates doing repetitive things so you can usually come up with something.

When you are finished, read what you wrote and circle everything that you think is science-related.

_____

_____

_____

_____

_____

_____

_____

_____

_____

_____

_____

_____

_____

_____

_____

_____

_____

_____

_____

_____

_____

_____

Topic Search: What Is the Problem?

Science solves problems. If you are looking for a solution to a problem that is important to you, then you will be more interested in the solution. Think of as many problems as you can that are encountered in your everyday life, such as getting up for school on time, remembering to do your homework, making your bedroom door stop squeaking and shut properly, etc. As you go through your day, take your science journal with you and write down any problems you have. After a few days, use the format below to organize the notes in your science journal.

Problem #___: _____

_____

Possible Solution A: _____

_____

Possible Solution B: _____

_____

Possible Solution C: _____

_____

_____

Problem #___: _____

_____

Possible Solution A: _____

_____

Possible Solution B: _____

_____

Possible Solution C: _____

_____

_____

Name _____ **Date** _____

Topic Search: What Do You Already Know?

The best science fair topics come from the stuff you already find interesting. Make a list of your hobbies and interests (such as taking care of pets, coin collecting, painting, playing baseball, inline skating, rock collecting). Then, make a list of things you *already know* about that activity and the things you *would like to know*. For example, if you are trying to learn how to use inline skates and you know that you fall down a lot, can you find a wheel size that is best for beginners? Or, is there a particular brand of adhesive bandages that helps your wounds heal faster? If you enjoy painting, is there a formula you can develop to make your own paint? Or, is there a brand of brushes that lasts longer than any other brand? The possibilities are endless!

Activity (hobby/interest)	What I know already	Problems I have/Things I want to know
1. My dog Spot	• Needs to be fed twice a day • Is really smart • Likes to bark	• Needs to learn tricks • Barks too much
2. Coin collecting	• I shouldn't glue coins. • Some coins are valuable. • My sister likes to look at my coin collection.	• Coins won't stay unless I use glue. • Figuring out which ones are valuable • Sometimes when my sister looks at the coins she smudges them.
3. _____	_____ _____ _____ _____	_____ _____ _____ _____
4. _____	_____ _____ _____ _____	_____ _____ _____ _____
5. _____	_____ _____ _____ _____	_____ _____ _____ _____

Activity (hobby/interest)	What I know already	Problems I have/Things I want to know
6. _____	_____	_____
	_____	_____
	_____	_____
	_____	_____
7. _____	_____	_____
	_____	_____
	_____	_____
	_____	_____
8. _____	_____	_____
	_____	_____
	_____	_____
	_____	_____
9. _____	_____	_____
	_____	_____
	_____	_____
	_____	_____
10. _____	_____	_____
	_____	_____
	_____	_____
	_____	_____

Almost anything you list in the third column can be turned into a science fair project. For example, how can you be sure your dog has cold water even when you are at school? There are lots of ways to make sure he has cold water and some ideas will work better than others. You might put water in the dog's dish and put the dish in the freezer every night before you go to bed. Then in the morning, fill the dish the rest of the way with water. The ice will slowly melt throughout the day. If there is water left when you get home, the dog had enough, or if the temperature is much cooler than a dish of regular water you have left out, the water is cooler. If you put a bowl of cold water out when you get home and he laps it up like he is really thirsty, you have to try something else.

Topic Search: What Do You See?

You can use a science project to solve problems in your home, school, or neighborhood. For example, suppose you live in an area that has periodic drought. When there is not enough rain, water restrictions mean people cannot water their lawns—everyone's grass dies. Can you do anything about how much rain is in your area? Probably not, but you might be able to help people by studying different kinds of grasses and showing that one species of grass needs less water. If the grass needs less water, it will survive drought conditions better. Local problems like this can make great, useful projects. Make a list of your own.

Location	Problem
Neighborhood	• The grass needs to be watered every day because there is not enough precipitation. • Little kids play too close to the street. • Cars go too fast down my street. • People put their garbage out. Stray dogs knock over the cans.
School	• Everyone has to wait outside before the doors open and sometimes it's too cold. • After school, there is a huge traffic jam outside the main door of the school. • There is always a huge group of kids standing in line for lunch. I never have enough time to eat after I get my lunch.

_____ _____

_____

_____

_____

_____ _____

_____

_____

_____

_____ _____

_____

_____

_____

Name _____   **Date** _____

Topic Search: Fill in the Blank!

This activity is just like freewriting, but with a little more direction. Do not put any limits on the kinds of things you write down. Even if something does not seem like a scientific idea at first, you may be able to turn it into a great experiment! Use more sheets of paper if necessary.

1. I wonder what would happen if I _____
   _____.

2. If I (do this) _____, then (I think this will happen)
   _____.

3. What effect does _____ have on
   _____?

4. What if _____ caused
   _____?

1. I wonder what would happen if I _____
   _____.

2. If I (do this) _____, then (I think this will happen)
   _____.

3. What effect does _____ have on
   _____?

4. What if _____ caused
   _____?

1. I wonder what would happen if I _____
   _____.

2. If I (do this) _____, then (I think this will happen)
   _____.

3. What effect does _____ have on
   _____?

4. What if _____ caused
   _____?

Topic Search: What Is Unusual About That?

Has something interesting happened to you? Sometimes an unusual experience you have had can become a good science fair topic. Write down the five most interesting things that have happened to you. Then, think about ways you can turn one of the events into a project.

_____

_____

_____

_____

_____

_____

_____

_____

_____

_____

_____

_____

_____

_____

_____

_____

_____

_____

_____

_____

_____

Turning a Topic into a Project

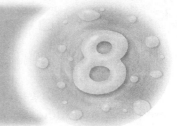

Now you need to turn that topic into a question, the question into a hypothesis, and the hypothesis into an experiment. But don't get overwhelmed! Fill in the blanks below to begin organizing your project.

1. My topic is: _____

2. The question I asked is: _____

_____

3. In short, this is how I want to study my topic: _____

_____

_____

4. Draw a check mark in the box if the sentence is true for your project.

☐   My question cannot be answered with "yes" or "no."

☐   I will be interested in this topic for the long haul.

☐   I will be able to complete this experiment at least two weeks before the science fair.

☐   I will be able to get the permission I need to do this.

☐   I will be able to get the equipment and resources necessary to complete my project.

☐   My school does not have any rules that will stop me from doing this project.

☐   I do not already know the answer to my question.

☐   I have specified the exact type of subjects for my experiment (the species of plant or animal, the breed of dog, etc.).

☐   I will be able to use more than one subject.

☐   I will be able to locate the subjects I need to use.

If each box does not have a check mark, you need to select another topic from the list you generated or work on the topic you selected a little more.

Research

Research, or gathering information from different sources to help you know more about your science project topic, is different with every experiment. For example, if you experiment with plants, you will want to research all about the plants you use, including their needs and their scientific names. If you work with chemicals, you may need to know the formulas of the chemicals, the amounts you are using and the brand names, if applicable. If you do a product comparison, you will want to know the differences between the various products you are testing, and you should know about any research that shows why the products were created as they were.

Use the following steps to make sure you have all your necessary research, but WRITE EVERYTHING IN YOUR INFORMAL SCIENCE JOURNAL!

1. Write down some observations in your science journal about your topic. (Remember, observations are things you notice with your senses. What color is it? What does it smell like? What does it look like? Does it move? What does it feel like? What have you seen it do? How does it act?)

2. What are some of the questions you have about your topic? For example, suppose you want to discover which dog treats dalmatians like best. The questions you might want to ask are: Are certain treats specified for certain breeds? How many different kinds of dog treats are there? Who can I talk to about dog treats so that I do not give the dogs too many or give them something that is not good for them? (Breeders, veterinarians, dalmatian owners, etc.) What ingredients go into dog treats? Why do the manufacturers of different dog treats claim their brand is the best? Have similar experiments been done on this topic? If so, what qualities did they test and what were the results? Are there any special precautions I need to take or safety equipment I need to do this project?

Documentation

After you know what kind of information you need to find, you will want to start looking through resources. Check the science fair rules (generally 3–8 sources are sufficient). You should use as many current sources as you can that are less than five years old because the content of information changes rapidly. Additionally, you should use a variety of sources such as magazines, journals, books, encyclopedias, and the Internet. Use the Documenting Sources worksheet (page 19) to record all the sources you use so it is possible for anyone who looks at your project to find the sources again.

If you have trouble finding information on your topic, it could be that your topic is too specific or that it has never been studied before. If the topic has never been studied, it might be exciting to discover something new. Get an opinion about the feasibility of your project from your science teacher. As long as you have a safe plan, go for it!

Documenting Sources

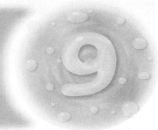

Record the following information for each source. Use as many copies of this page as needed.

Title of the book, magazine, newspaper, Web site: _____

_____

Copyright date: _____

Title of article: _____

Author: _____

Publisher/Web site sponsor: _____

Pages: _____

Summary: (Write down the useful information.) _____

_____

_____

_____

Title of the book, magazine, newspaper, Web site: _____

_____

Copyright date: _____

Title of article: _____

Author: _____

Publisher/Web site sponsor: _____

Pages: _____

Summary: (Write down the useful information.) _____

_____

_____

_____

Hypothesis

The hypothesis is a testable statement that you make as an answer to the question you have about your topic. This statement is important because it will be used to guide the entire experiment. The hypothesis can be stated as an "if—then" statement. "If I do this, then (I think) this will happen." So you can say, "If I give two dalmatians a choice between two brands of dog treats, they will prefer brand X (name of brand) over brand Y (name of brand)." The hypothesis also gives the relationship between two variables (the independent and dependent variables) in your experiment. So before you write your hypothesis, you need to understand more about what the variables are.

Variable

A variable is anything that affects your topic and can change in your experiment. If you were studying a specific type of plant, variables could include air temperature, soil type, container size, the material the container is made from, amount of sunlight, amount and type of water, and so forth. Anything that can help or harm the plant is a variable.

Independent Variable

The independent variable is the one thing that you change in your experiment to figure out what impact it has on the topic you study. If you wanted to find out what treat dalmatians prefer, you would have to offer the treats to the dogs at approximately the same time of day, put the treat at the same distance from each dog, be sure that each dog is fed about the same time every day, and find dog treats that are about the same size and consistency (hard, soft, chewy). These are all variables that you would need to control. The one thing that you should change is the brand of treat being offered to the dog. The brand is the independent variable. This is the one thing that you will deliberately change.

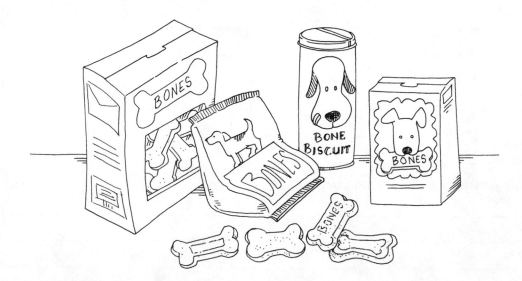

Dependent Variable

When you change one factor (the independent variable), you will watch what happens to the rest of your experiment. What happens is called the dependent variable. The dependent variable is the factor of your experiment that changes as a result of the independent variable. How will you know which brand of dog treats the dogs prefer? Which brand gets munched down first? If you were comparing two brands of similar dog treats, you would expect that the dogs would eat their favorite kind of dog treat first. So, the treat which was eaten first would be the dependent variable.

Control Group

As you plan your variables, you need to try to include a group of test subjects that will demonstrate how the experiment will work when the independent variable is not applied. This is known as the control group.

Experimental Group

The group of test subjects that you use to show what happens when the independent variable is applied is called the experimental group. You should plan to measure both results in your data if possible. Then it is clear what changes are caused by the independent variable. In the case of the dog treats, if the dogs have been eating one of the brands all along, you would have to time the dogs to see how long they took to eat that brand for the control group, then give them the old and new kinds to see which kind was eaten first and how long it took for the experimental group.

Beginning Your Experiment Plan

Use the following information to record the variables and hypothesis in your informal journal.

Variables

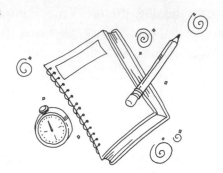

1. List all the variables you will need to consider in your experiment:

_____

_____

_____

2. What is the independent variable in your experiment? (What are you going to test?)

_____

3. What is the dependent variable? (What will change as a result of the independent variable?)

_____

Hypothesis

Write some If–Then statements in the spaces below, thinking about the variables you listed above and which ones you should test. For example: If I do this (state your independent variable), then this will happen (state how your dependent variable will change).

1. If _____,

   then _____.

2. The hypothesis of my experiment is that _____will

   cause _____.

3. I hypothesize that if I _____then

   will result.

4. In my experiment, I hypothesized that there would be a direct relationship between _____

   _____and

   _____.

5. If I _____,

   then _____.

Materials List and Getting the Materials

After you have written your hypothesis and listed the variables you plan to test, it should become obvious what equipment you will use to do your experiment. Make a list of the supplies you will need in your journal, then have an adult help you decide how to get all of your materials. When you are finished, write your list over again neatly and then check off each item as you get it. Here are some guidelines:

- **Try to include exact measurements** as soon as possible. Instead of listing "water," list "water, 100 milliliters."
- **Do not forget to list your measuring tools** as part of the materials list. All measurements should be metric, so all your measuring tools should have metric increments.
- **List the safety equipment.** Chemicals require a chemical apron and gloves. Most experiments require goggles. Heat requires hot pads. Open flame, stoves, or other electric appliances require adult supervision!
- **Include brand names** whenever possible, even if you are not testing properties of a specific brand.
- As you proceed, remember that you will probably think of items that were not included on the list. **Just add items as they come to you.**
- **Store your equipment in one place.** Often it is helpful to place it in a labeled, cardboard box with a lid you can close. The exceptions to this are items which need to be kept warm or cold, or items which are poisonous, such as chemicals (these should be kept in a safe area designated by an adult).
- **Make sure you get enough materials for two rounds of experiments.** Having enough will prevent extra shopping trips. It will also save you from not being able to get the same brand name of anything you need (which would create an independent variable you did not consider).
- **Obtain approval from your science teacher for your project.** If you plan to experiment with animals (and have obtained school permission), it is not a bad idea to list what the animal eats and drinks each day during the experiment, even if that is not what you are testing. Check with your science teacher to see if this is necessary.

Data

All experiments require data. Data are the results of your experiment, but they are written in such a way, either in the form of a chart or graph, that shows at a glance how you measured your results. You will want to quantify the results by measuring some factors such as time, temperature, volume, height, weight, mass, and so forth.

It is important to plan how you will measure your results before you start the experiment. The way you measure your data will be determined by the way you perform your experiment, and you will need to record results over the time you are doing your experiment. Also, if possible, remember to measure the results from the control group as well as the experimental group. This will show more clearly what happens when the independent variable is applied.

Examples:
I will use a metric ruler to measure the height of the tulip every day.
I will use a balance to get the mass of the marble block every day.

Using Graphs

As you plan the experiment, you must decide what you will measure and how you will explain your data. **Circle graphs** (also called pie charts) are used to show portions of an amount, as well as how a part's share relates to the whole. Each "slice" of the circle graph shows a percent of the whole. You cannot show how two variables are related using a circle graph.

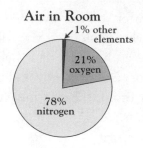

Air in Room

1% other elements

21% oxygen

78% nitrogen

Bar graphs are used to compare quantities which do not continually change. Just as the name implies, bars are used. Suppose you want to compare the height of four people. The independent variable is always placed on the *x*-axis. You chose the scale by looking at the highest and lowest numbers. People's heights do not usually change very rapidly, at least not from day to day. In the example experiment with fertilizer, a bar graph would be a poor choice because you would only have two bars, one for the control group and one for the experimental group.

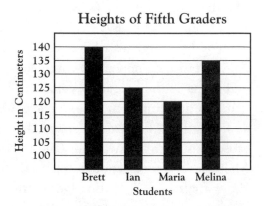

Heights of Fifth Graders

Line graphs are used to show how one variable in an experiment responds to the change in another. Pairs of numbers are used to express a relationship between the dependent and independent variable. In a line graph, the independent variable is placed on the *x*-axis (horizontal) and the dependent variable goes on the *y*-axis (vertical axis). Line graphs are most often used because they can help you answer the hypothesis, your "if-then" question, by showing you patterns in your data. Unlike circle and bar graphs, you can plot many sets of data on one graph. In the example experiment on fertilizer, the line graph would be the best choice because you could quickly get a picture of how your independent variable (addition of fertilizer) affected the dependent variable (height of grass). There would be two lines on the graph, one for the control group and one for the experimental group.

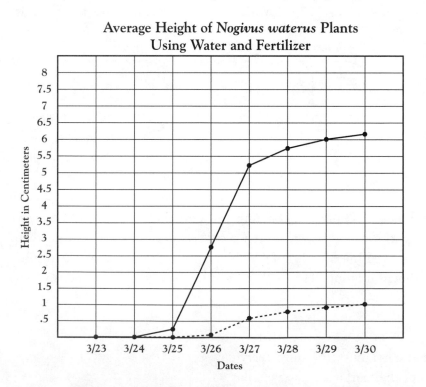

Average Height of *Nogivus waterus* Plants Using Water and Fertilizer

Procedure

When you write your procedure, you will write out what you are going to do and EXACTLY how you are going to do it in a step-by-step format. Pretend you are explaining it to someone over the telephone, so that the impulse we often have to "just show them" is not there. Or, imagine trying to explain how to conduct your experiment to someone who has no idea what your experiment is. It might even help to imagine that the person to whom you are explaining the experiment is a few years younger than you are. If you have a younger sibling, try telling him/her about your idea and then think about the questions he/she asks you.

Example:

OK	NOT OK
1. Using a 250 mL beaker, measure 1 liter of water.	1. Add water to beaker.
2. Pour the water slowly from the 250 mL beaker into the 1 liter container.	2. Pour water into other container.
3. Let the water stand until it is at room temperature (about 22° Celsius).	3. Use warm water.

Why so detailed? Another person should be able to pick up your research and do exactly what you did the same way you did it. That is how scientists verify each other's work. If another person can duplicate your experiment and get the exact results you did, then you did a good job explaining your procedure. After duplicating your experiment, the other person might want to build on your research. Each researcher who studies the topic adds little bits and pieces to our understanding of the topic until amazing things are discovered.

When you design your experiment, refer to the example experiment on page 26, then use the worksheet on page 27 to write out the procedure you plan to use to conduct your experiment.

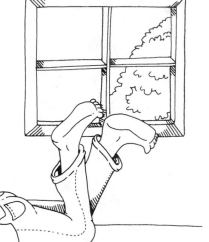

Remember, all the time you are completing each step, you will also be writing the observations in your informal journal. If you write out the experiment and make changes, be sure to record them in your journal. Do not stop keeping detailed notes as you near the time to perform the experiment.

How Does Your Grass Grow?

Question: How effective is the use of fertilizer to increase the growth of Nebraska Green® grass?

Hypothesis: If fertilizer is added to water and given to Nebraska Green® grass (Nogivus waterus) everyday, the grass will grow taller.

Materials: 10 plastic pots that are 2 cm high and 5 cm wide, 5 liters of Grow Good® soil, permanent marker, Grow Fast Fertilizer, electronic balance (accurate to one one-hundredth of a decimal), graduated cylinder, Drink Right® bottled water, 500 mL beaker, Nebraska Green® grass (Nogivus waterus) seed, flat toothpick, thermometer, stirring rod, goggles, plastic apron

Procedure:
1. Divide the ten pots into two groups of five. Mark one group of pots with the permanent marker as the "control group" and the second set of five pots as the "experimental group."
2. Use the 500 mL graduated cylinder to add 500 mL of Grow Good® potting soil to each pot.
3. Add ten grass seeds to each pot so that the seeds are 1 cm apart on all sides. Use the flat toothpick to push the seeds down 1 cm into the soil.
4. Pour 500 mL of Drink Right® water into the clean beaker. Use the balance to mass out exactly 20 grams of fertilizer. Add the fertilizer to the water and stir for one minute.
5. Add 50 mL of Drink Right® water to each of the control group pots. Add 50 mL of Drink Right® water *with fertilizer* to each of the experimental group pots.
6. Place all 10 pots in a south-facing window.
7. Each day, measure the height of each plant and divide by the number of plants to get the average height of the grass plants in each pot.
8. Record in the informal journal the amount of sunlight the plants receive each day and the temperature of the room.
9. Add 50 mL of water to the control group pots each week and 50 mL of the fertilizer solution to the experimental pots each week.

Planning the Procedure

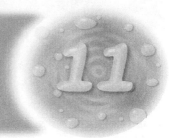

1. List your materials here (Don't forget safety equipment):

_____

_____

_____

_____

2. Plan how you will measure your results:

_____

_____

_____

_____

_____

_____

_____

_____

_____

3. List each step of your procedure in order:

_____

_____

_____

_____

_____

_____

_____

_____

_____

Record Keeping

During the experiment, keep a log of daily observations in your informal journal. You do not want to make decisions now about what is important to write, just write everything that you observe. You can choose only the most important stuff to use in your report later.

For example:

Date	Observation
3/23	I planted the seeds today.
3/24	Nothing yet
3/25	Fifteen of the seeds in the experimental group germinated. I can see the grass starting to poke through the soil.
3/26	All the seeds in the experimental group germinated. Only 20 seeds in the control group germinated. The control grass looks white and the experimental grass is green.
3/27	All of the control seeds germinated. The grass is visible above the soil but the control grass is a much lighter color than the experimental grass. The experimental grass is taller and greener.
3/28	The control grass grew slightly, only 2 millimeters. The experimental grass also grew slowly, only 4 millimeters.
3/29	The experimental grass is still a lot taller and greener than the control.
3/30	The experimental grass is a lot taller today. Some of the blades in the control grass are starting to turn a little brown on the edges. I added 20 mL of water to the control grass and 20 mL of water and fertilizer to the experimental grass today.

You will also want to have a table of your measurements. Be sure to make very accurate measurements and include the unit in your journal.

Date	Average Height in Centimeters	
	Control	Experimental
3/23	0	0
3/24	0	0
3/25	0	0.3
3/26	0.2	3.0
3/27	0.6	5.2
3/28	0.8	5.8
3/29	0.9	6.0
3/30	1.0	6.2

For each set of data, you will probably want to have a table. For your observations, a table is enough. For your measurements, you will need a graph because a graph shows the patterns and trends in the data better. The type of graph you use will depend on the type of data you collected because a graph is really just a picture of your data. (See page 24 for examples of graphs.)

Staying on Schedule

If your experiment lasts for more than a week and has tasks you must remember to perform each day, it may be difficult to stay on schedule. If you forget to do a part of your experiment on any given day (water plants, feed animals, etc.), it can affect your results.

In order to help you remember to stay on schedule, create a Daily Experiment Schedule to plan the parts of your experiment. Make at least two copies of it. Keep one copy at school and refer to it each day before you go home so that you will remember to keep track of what you should be doing. Post the other copy in a prominent place at home, such as on your bedroom door or on the refrigerator, so that you will have a reminder for after school and on the weekends.

If you forget to do part of your experiment, you have two choices. One is to do the forgotten task as soon as you remember, then acknowledge the schedule change in your notes and conclusion. The other is to start the experiment over again.

Troubleshooting

Science works great when everything functions according to plan but what if something goes wrong? If something goes wrong in your experiment, make a note of it in your conclusion. Sometimes you can correct the problem and just start all over. Suppose in the example experiment, the grass in the control actually grew better. What would you do then? Fudge the results? Never change your data! A hypothesis is not like a question on a test, you do not lose credit for being wrong. *In fact, disproving your hypothesis can lead to some fascinating discoveries and will actually improve your project.* Everyone will have more respect for you if you admit your errors and if you are curious enough to keep wondering why. Remember, penicillin was discovered by accident and has saved countless lives.

Name _____   **Date** _____

The Results and Conclusion

Explaining the Results

After you have conducted your experiment (preferably twice), you will know what happened in the experiment. These are your results, and you can communicate them to other people through the data you show in a graph or table. In the results section, you should only present a simple, factual summary of what happened in the experiment. You can elaborate on what happened in the conclusion section.

Examples:

The experimental group of plants grew an average of 1.5 cm taller than the control group.

The dalmatians ate brand X (name of brand) dog treats first on 10 out of 14 days.

1. When you applied your independent variable, what happened to the dependent variable?

_____

_____

_____

2. Write a brief summary of the result.

_____

_____

_____

_____

The Conclusion

What happened? What went right? What went wrong? What would you do differently, and what did you learn? This is the not the same as the results or the data. It's your opinion and some observations about those two elements. The conclusion is stated at the end of your report.

Use this worksheet to figure out how to write your conclusion. Write your comments in your journal if you need more space.

1. Were your results consistent? (Did it always happen that way?)

_____

_____

The Conclusion (continued)

2. Is there anything else that could have caused the change in the dependent variable?

_____

_____

_____

_____

3. Explain any problems and how you would correct them in the future.

_____

_____

_____

_____

4. Explain what you would do differently if you did this experiment again.

_____

_____

_____

_____

5. Discuss how your results were different from what you expected.

_____

_____

_____

_____

6. Discuss other questions you have now that your experiment is finished.

_____

_____

_____

_____

The Written Report

When you are finished, it's time to take information from your informal journal, including the results and data, and create a typed, neat, thorough report. You cannot use any of the worksheets for the report. It must be a new document, created by you (with some help if you need it). The written report should have the following sections:

Title Page

- The project title
- Your name
- School name
- School address
- Your grade in school

The title is the first thing most people will see, so make your title sound interesting.

Table of Contents

List all parts of the report along with the page numbers.

Abstract

- 250 words or less
- State the hypothesis.
- A summary of the purpose of your project
- Generalized data
- What was learned

Introduction

- State the hypothesis.
- Explain how you got your idea.
- Explain your topic.
- Include important information from your research.
- Explain what you hoped to achieve in your project.

Experimental Procedures

- Write exactly what you did and how you did it. This part should be so detailed that a child two years younger than you could get the same results.
- Explain what equipment you used and include size, brand, and type.
- Avoid using first person pronouns such as I or me.

Data

- A table with your daily observations
- The data table with your daily measurements
- Charts and graphs made from the measurements using a computer program.

Results

- Provide information on what happened during the experiment. You are just reporting information.
- Summarize the results of your experiment.

Conclusion

- Explain any problems and how you would correct them in the future.
- Explain what you would do differently if you did this experiment again.
- Discuss how your results were different from what you expected.
- Discuss other questions you have now that you did this experiment.

References

- Use bibliography format to list any books, articles, businesses, or professionals that provided you with information.

Acknowledgments

- Give credit to anyone who helped with your experiment.
- Thank anyone who helped you with supplies or expenses.

The Effect of Grow-Fast® Fertilizer On the Height of *Nogivus waterus*

Pamela J. Galus
Realgood Middle School
120 Anywhere Street
Omaha, NE 0X0XX
Sixth Grade

Table of Contents

2

Abstract

The purpose of my project was to determine if fertilizer would benefit the most common type of grass planted in my area, *Nogivus waterus*. My hypothesis is that if I give fertilizer to one group of *Nogivus waterus* plants, then that group would grow taller. I determined that my hypothesis was correct. The *Nogivus waterus* plants that received water with added fertilizer grew taller an average of 5.2 cm than the control plants that did not receive the fertilizer. In addition, the grass that received the fertilizer had a deeper green color and did not turn brown, as did the grass in the control group.

3

Introduction

My hypothesis is: If fertilizer is added to water and given to Nebraska Green® grass (*Nogivus waterus*) every day, the grass will grow taller.

I got this idea from watching my father fertilize the yard. He told me that fertilizing the yard costs money but it made the grass grow better. Therefore, I wanted to show that my father was not wasting time and money when he fertilized the grass, because the fertilizer really does help the grass grow better. My control group was given plain water. My experimental group received fertilizer mixed in water according to the directions on the package.

4

Experimental Procedure

Question: Does fertilizer increase the growth of Nebraska Green® grass?

Hypothesis: If fertilizer is added to water and given to Nebraska Green® grass (*Nogivus waterus*) everyday, the grass will grow taller.

Materials: 10 plastic pots that are 2 cm high and 5 cm wide, 5 liters of Grow Good® soil, permanent marker, Grow Fast® fertilizer, electronic balance (accurate to one one-hundredth of a decimal), graduated cylinder, Drink Right® bottled water, 500 mL beaker, Nebraska Green® grass (*Nogivus waterus*) seed, flat toothpick, thermometer, stirring rod, goggles, plastic apron

Procedure:
1. Divide the ten pots into two groups of five. Mark one group of pots with the permanent marker as the "control group" and the second set of five pots as the "experimental group."
2. Use the 500 mL graduated cylinder to add 500 mL of Grow Good® potting soil to each pot.
3. Add ten grass seeds to each pot so that the seeds are 1 cm apart on all sides. Use the flat toothpick to push the seeds down 1 cm into the soil.
4. Pour 500 mL of Drink Right® water into the clean beaker. Use the balance to mass out exactly 20 grams of fertilizer. Add the fertilizer to the water and stir for one minute.
5. Add 50 mL of Drink Right® water to each of the control group pots. Add 50 mL of Drink Right® water *with fertilizer* to each of the experimental group pots.
6. Place all 10 pots in a south-facing window.
7. Each day, measure the height of each plant and divide by the number of plants to get the average height of the grass plants in each pot.
8. Record in the informal journal the amount of sunlight the plants receive each day and the temperature of the room.
9. Add 50 mL of water to the control group pots each week and 50 mL of the fertilizer solution to the experimental pots each week.

5

The Data

Date	Observation
3/23	I planted the seeds today.
3/24	Nothing yet
3/25	Fifteen of the seeds in the experimental group germinated and I can see the grass starting to poke through the soil.
3/26	All the seeds in the experimental group germinated. Only 20 seeds in the control group germinated. The control grass looks white and the experimental grass is green.
3/27	All of the control seeds germinated. The grass is visible above the soil but the control grass is a much lighter color than the experimental grass. The experimental grass is taller and greener.
3/28	The control grass grew slightly—only 2 millimeters. The experimental grass also grew slowly—only 4 millimeters.
3/29	The experimental grass is still a lot taller and greener than the control.
3/30	The experimental grass is a lot taller today. Some of the blades in the control grass are starting to turn a little brown on the edges. I added 20 mL of water to the control group and 20 mL of water and fertilizer to the experimental group today.

Date	Average Height in Centimeters	
	Control	Experimental
3/23	0	0
3/24	0	0
3/25	0	0
3/26	0.2	3.0
3/27	0.6	5.2
3/28	0.8	5.8
3/29	0.9	6.0
3/30	1.0	6.2

6

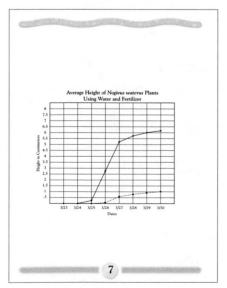

Average Height of *Nogivus waterus* Plants Using Water and Fertilizer

7

Results

In this experiment, the control group did not grow as tall or as fast as the experimental group. Also, some of the blades of the control group started to turn a little brown on the edges and at the tips. On average, the experimental group grew 5.2 cm taller than the control group.

8

Conclusion

I used the toothpick to push the seeds beneath the soil, but some seeds came to the top when I added the water and the water/fertilizer. I reread the procedure direction and realized that it said I should push them down 1 inch. I only pushed the seeds 1 cm below the soil. I did not pay any attention to the unit then, but now I know that I should have pushed them 2.54 cm below the soil.

When I was doing this experiment, I started to wonder what would happen if I did another experiment. Only this time, I would give the control group fertilizer mixed according to the package directions and the experimental group would get fertilizer solution mixed twice as strong. If some fertilizer were good, maybe more would be better.

The grass that I used, *Nogivus waterus*, needs less water than some other types of grass. Since our state does not get much rainfall, this type of grass is very popular here. I wondered what would have happened to the plants if I had reduced the amount of water both groups received. It kind of started to look like the control grass was too wet because it was not growing as fast as the experimental group. I do not think that fast-growing grass should be the goal, but rather grass that does not need as much water or other care, such as mowing and fertilizing. If my father does not spend as much time on the lawn, he will have more time to play kickball with my friends and me. Therefore, I would like to find out what would be the easiest way to grow healthy, easy-care grass.

9

Creating the Display

You worked hard making your project the best it can be. The display is how you communicate your hard work to the judges. The display has three parts:

1. The written report.

2. Objects and/or equipment that you used during the experiment—anything that will help people understand your project. *Check the guidelines provided by your teacher because some science fairs only allow pictures of your experiments.* If your experiment involved taking surveys of children. Permissions must be signed by the children's parents and included in the formal journal. The judges will ask to see those permissions. Also if you plan on using photographs of the children who participated, separate permissions must also be obtained from the parents.

3. The back board is used to tell the story of your entire experiment. The back board can be purchased at a craft or hobby store. It is usually sold as a board that has three sections (trifold) hooked together so it can be folded for ease of moving. You can also make your board out of poster board or even plywood. Whatever you use, your display board should be able to stand alone. *Check the rules of the science fair for the size of the display.* Your display board can usually be smaller, but not larger, than the dimensions given in the rules.

Special Suggestions for a Eye-Catching Display

- Use a computer, stencils, or stick-on letters. Use a dark color for the title so it will stand out more.
- Make the letters for the title the largest letters on your board.
- Paste the letters on construction paper on your board. You will be able to take the construction paper off and redo a section.
- Do not use more than three different colors. Use colors that go well together. Your display should look attractive.
- Place your written report and formal journal in front of your backboard.

Tips for a Successful Presentation

For some people, the oral presentation is the hardest and scariest part of the science fair. Usually, schools arrange it so that you will stand next to your project, and people will come over and ask you to tell them about it. People come individually or in groups. Don't be nervous about a lot of people. More people means lots of interest, and that's good!

It is very important that you practice your oral presentation several times before you go to the fair, because everyone gets a little nervous and it can be hard to remember what to say. Put brief notes onto index cards that will help you remember what you want to say, in what order. Do not write complete sentences on the cards, because then you will want to read directly from the cards.

The best thing to do is to practice in front of a mirror or stuffed animal a few times. When you feel that you are ready for a live audience, practice in front of your parents, then ask them if they have suggestions to help you improve. You might want to videotape yourself so you can see areas you want to fix.

Time for Judging

Dress for success on the day of the science fair. You will feel more confident if you look your best. As you speak, use correct speaking skills.

During the judging, stay with your project, and use it to help you remember important details. Have your note cards nearby in case you forget what to say. If you get confused or cannot remember the information, take a deep breath and try to relax. If someone gives advice, thank the person for the input but do not argue. However, you can explain why you did things the way you did them. The judges may not agree with you, but they may understand your line of thinking better.

If you do not know an answer to a question, be honest and admit you do not know the answer. The judges will know if you are faking your answers. You may also want to tell the judges what you think the answer might be based on all that you have learned, but make sure you tell them it is only an educated guess.

Things to Remember

- Use proper English and avoid slang.
- Know your topic.
- Do not memorize a speech. Think of this as a talk about your work.
- Have resources and notes available but do not read off of anything.
- Use your display as a guide to help you remember what to say.
- Speak loudly and clearly.
- Speak slowly so you will not appear nervous.
- If you are nervous, admit it. (It will help you relax).
- Smile and be enthusiastic.
- Look at the audience.
- Stand up straight. (You worked hard and have a right to be proud of your project).
- Do not chew gum or eat candy.
- Be courteous and polite.

What Are the Judges Thinking?

The judges will ask themselves the following questions about each part of your experiment. They may ask you the questions as well, so think about how you would answer each question. When you think of your answers, don't just stop with "yes" or "no." Be ready to explain yourself.

The Topic and Question

1. Does the project try to solve a real problem? Is the solution useful to anyone?
2. Were you truly interested in finding the answer to this question? Why?
3. Is the project creative and original?
4. Did you use good problem-solving techniques?
5. Did the experiment have clearly-defined objectives? What were they?
6. Was the problem limited enough so that you could find a workable solution?

The Data

1. Are graphs labeled properly and titled?
2. Are all measurements listed in metric units?
3. Are the data accurate?
4. Are the data interpreted correctly?
5. Are the data displayed correctly?
6. Are there limitations in the data? If so, what are they?
7. What was the most creative part of the way you collected and analyzed the data?
8. Was the sample large enough to make the data useful?

The Experiment Design

1. What are the creative elements of the way you designed your experiment?
2. Does the experiment show careful planning of time requirements and design?
3. Was the equipment used correctly?
4. Was safety equipment used correctly? Were safety procedures followed?

5. What were the dependent and independent variables?
6. Were all of the variables recognized?
7. Were all variables controlled except for the one being studied?
8. Did you design a project that was within your means to execute?
9. What kind of teacher/parent/friend help did you need? Did you ask for too much help, or were you able to work mostly independently?

The Research

1. Did you use a variety of research? Are your sources credible (not just popular literature)? Are they up-to-date (less than five years old)?
2. Did you talk to experts in the community?
3. Did you use both printed and electronic sources?
4. Are all sources cited correctly? Are direct quotes used where needed?

General Questions

1. If anything unusual happened, what new questions came to mind that could be investigated?
2. Were the data used to draw a logical and appropriate conclusion?
3. Does the conclusion show a thorough understanding of the topic?
4. Do you have a sufficient understanding of the project to talk knowledgeably about it?
5. Is anything left out of the project that should be included?
6. Has other research been done on this project?

EXPERIMENTS

Why have experiments in this book if you are expected to come up with your own?

These experiments are NOT meant to be the exact ones you use for your science project! They are not all-inclusive of all the areas of science, either. Your project will be much better and more fun if you pick a topic that interests you! These experiments are meant to help you understand the scientific process, and maybe to help you come up with even better, creative, unique ideas of your own! Also note: some of these experiments are often used in actual science classrooms. So, if you copy one of these exactly, it may look familiar to the judges!

Should I do the experiments or just read them?

That is up to you, but doing a practice experiment that interests you may help you come up with your own idea. It will certainly help you with the scientific process.

Some of the equipment might be hard to get. How do I get it?

Since data should be measured as precisely as possible, many of these experiments will require a balance, graduated cylinder, or other metric measuring device. Balances can often be purchased at a department store or health food store. (These are sold to dieters who measure their food portions by weight.) Graduated cylinders can be replaced with syringes that have the needles removed. (Purchase these at a medical supply store or ask a medical professional.) If you need something that proves hard to find, ask your science teacher for help.

What if I have a problem doing one of the experiments in this book?

The experiment suggestions include a wide variety of difficulty levels. Some are easy and some are hard. You should definitely inform an adult about what experiment you want to do, and have supervision during the experiment, or at least have an adult nearby who can help if needed. If you have a problem arise that is not dangerous, try to look at it as a challenge to use creativity to solve it. A problem in an experiment from this book could lead to an idea for an original experiment that you can do yourself.

What about safety issues?

Before you start any experiment, get adult permission and arrange for an adult to be around the entire time while you do your experiment. Also keep these things in mind:

- It is recommended that you wear protective eyewear (goggles) during your experiment if you are working with chemicals and anything else that may be hazardous.
- If you have allergies or asthma, get adult permission to use chemicals with strong odors or grow a bacteria sample, and always have any necessary medication on hand.
- Young children and pets should be kept away from bacteria, small or sharp objects, and chemicals. Make sure your experimentation area is safe and secure!
- IF YOU ARE USING HUMAN OR ANIMAL SUBJECTS, GET SCHOOL PERMISSION FIRST. Treat all live subjects with care and respect.

Brrrr . . . Bubbles

BACKGROUND

Most kids like to blow bubbles, and truthfully, most older people do too! But they pop pretty quickly. You might want to try to keep bubbles around so you can enjoy them longer. To do that, you would have to think about all the things that affect a bubble and what types of things you could change to make it last longer. Then, you would test one thing at a time until you found the way to make the longest lasting bubble. You would have to think about things like bubble ingredients (type of soap, type of water, other added ingredients such as sugar and glycerine), temperature, wind, light, bubble size, bubble shape, and more. There is a whole lot of science to bubble blowing and it makes a great project because everybody from the very young to the very old, love bubbles.

QUESTION

How does temperature affect the longevity of soap bubbles?

RESEARCH TOPICS

Bubble, soap, temperature, heat, diffraction, air pressure, light

HYPOTHESIS

Bubbles blown in a cold environment will last longer than bubbles blown in a warm environment.

MATERIALS

Goggles, 250 mL liquid detergent (be sure to record the brand you use), 720 mL distilled water, 12 mL glycerine, bubble wand (can be purchased at a toy store or fashioned from wire), hot water bottle, ice pack, 10 gallon (45.46 L) aquarium with a solid lid, graduated cylinder, bucket, alcohol aquarium thermometer, two drinking straws in paper wrappers, small jar, tape, clock with secondhand, bucket

PROCEDURE

1. Put on your goggles. Mix 250 mL of detergent, 720 mL distilled water, 12 mL of glycerine in the bucket. Dip the wand into the solution. If you do not get good bubbles, add more soap or another milliliter of glycerine. The glycerine prevents the bubbles from drying out as fast but adding too much will not make better bubbles.
2. Tape the thermometer in the center of a clean, dry aquarium. Pour the hot water into the hot water bottle and then place it inside the aquarium.
3. Put 30 mL of the soap solution in the bottom of the small jar. After 10 minutes, remove the hot water bottle and place the small jar with the bubble solution in the aquarium.
4. Tape the two straws together to make one long straw. Insert the straws through the lid so that the lid remains on the aquarium. The tip of the straws should be in the bubble solution.
5. Read the thermometer and record the temperature. Fill your lungs with air and blow into the straw for three seconds. Remove the straw quickly and time how long the bubbles last.

6. Repeat the same procedure for the ice pack.
7. Repeat the procedure for room temperature.

Longevity of Soap Bubbles

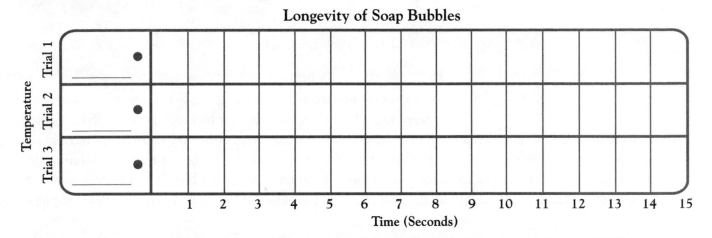

Temperature

Trial 1

Trial 2

Trial 3

1   2   3   4   5   6   7   8   9   10   11   12   13   14   15

Time (Seconds)

Hints: A bubble wand can be made from a straw with a loop of string on the end or a wire bent with a circle on the end. Using the aquarium keeps the air flow variable relatively constant. A large jar or beaker could also be used and the jar could then be placed in hot water or cold water baths to change the temperature. Count seconds until the last bubble with a diameter of at least one centimeter has popped. Try to blow the same number of bubbles each time by blowing with about the same force. By using your own exhaled breath for the bubbles, you are controlling the internal temperature as well as the mixture of gases present in each bubble for each trial.

TAKING IT FURTHER *Which bubble solution makes the best bubbles?* Instead of glycerine, try making bubbles with soap, water, sugar, corn starch or maybe just soap and water. Try different types of soaps and detergents, as well as other ingredients until you find the best mix for long-lasting bubbles. Then create a bubble stand (a loop of wire attached to a block of wood) so that the bubble film can be displayed and the various bubble solutions compared.

How does the shape of the bubble maker affect the shape of the bubbles? How would you find out if it is possible to blow square bubbles?

How does hard water affect the longevity of bubbles? If hard water is not available, it can be made by adding four antacid tablets that contain calcium carbonate to 250 mL of distilled water. Use the hard water to make one set of bubbles and distilled water to make another set and then compare the durability and longevity of the bubbles using the same bubble solution ingredients for each.

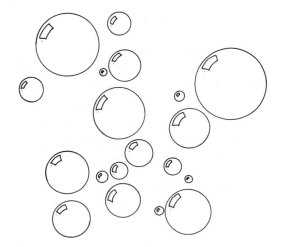

Building with Wood

Physical Science

BACKGROUND

Have you ever wanted to build something but you were not sure what material to use? Builders have that problem all the time. Even making a wood structure is not an easy decision. There are as many different types of wood as there are trees plus a few wood products people have created by blending different woods. Cost is often one of the factors that people take into consideration when deciding what wood to use. If you have two wood blocks that are the same size but one is heavier than the other, it might cost more and be more difficult to move the heavier piece.

If the heavier piece would make the structure more durable, it might still be a better choice. Density is the mass of an object divided by its volume. An object that is very dense has more matter in a given space. So if the two blocks are the same size but one is heavier, the heavier one is denser.

QUESTION

How is the density of wood related to its strength?

RESEARCH TOPICS

Wood (specific types used and what they are used for), density

HYPOTHESIS

If wood blocks are cut the same size, the heavier blocks will be stronger.

MATERIALS

Goggles, wood samples (that are relatively thin—for example, 20 cm x 1 cm x .5 cm), ruler, weights of different sizes, balance, calculator, string

PROCEDURE

1. Measure the exact length, width, and height of all the wood pieces and calculate the volume (L x W x H). Record the information on the data table.
2. Mass each sample using the balance and record the mass to two decimal places. Calculate the density of each wood sample (Density = mass ÷ volume)
3. Put on your goggles. Tape the ends of each wood sample securely between two tables. Use the string to suspend weights from the center of each wood piece. The weight should be about 5 cm above the floor so that the wood can bend. Be sure to keep your head and hands clear so that you will not be injured when the wood snaps.
4. Record the maximum weight each piece of wood can hold without cracking.

How Is the Density of Wood Related to Its Strength?

Wood Type	Length	Width	Height	Mass	Volume	Density

Hints: The wood can be cut to any size but the wood pieces tested should be as close as possible to the same size. A bar graph would be the best way to show the data in this experiment. Instead of weights, a small bucket suspended with string from each piece of wood can be used. Add equal masses of sand, a small amount at a time, to the bucket.

TAKING IT FURTHER In what other ways could the strength of wood be tested? Try this: press small wood blocks in a vice until an imprint is left in the wood.

How could you test the strength of a bridge design, rather than testing the strength of the wood?

Name _____   **Date** _____

Trust Metal to Rust

Physical Science

BACKGROUND

You know that cars rust, but have you ever noticed that different parts of the car start to rust first? Look at your family's car to see if rust is visible and make a note of the location of the rust. Generally, older cars will have more rust. After you have noted the places that cars tend to rust first, you will have to think about all the things that might cause cars to rust in those places. For example, when your parents drive on wet streets the tread on the tires may bring water up as they spin and get the underside of the car wet. If the car rusts more on the underside, it might be because that part of the car is wet more often.

QUESTION

How does wet weather affect the rate that cars rust?

RESEARCH TOPICS

Rust, iron, oxidation, galvanization

HYPOTHESIS

An iron nail placed in water will rust faster and lose more mass than a nail placed in sand.

MATERIALS

Two glass jars with 200 mL (baby food jars work but be sure to record volume, diameter, and height), balance, 10 iron nails (use the largest nails you can find and record the size), 200 mL of distilled water, 200 mL of very dry sand, beaker, paper towels

PROCEDURE

Day 1:
1. Place 200 mL of distilled water in one jar.
2. Place 200 mL of sand in a separate jar.
3. Use the balance to find the mass of the five nails. Record the mass on your data table. Place the nails in the jar of water.
4. Use the balance to find the mass of the other five nails. Record the mass on your data table. Place the second group of nails in the jar with the sand.

Day 2:
5. Get four paper towels. Write water on one paper towel. Take the nails out of the water jar. Place the nails on a paper towel. Pat the nails with a paper towel to remove excess water (do not rub the nails).
6. Write sand on the second paper towel. Take the nails out of the sand jar. Remove excess sand. (Do not rub the nails.)
7. Place the nails from the water jar on the balance. Record the mass on your data table. Put the nails back on the correctly labeled paper towel.

8. Place the nails from the sand jar on the balance. Record the mass on your data table. Put the nails back on the correctly labeled paper towel.
9. Return the nails from the paper towel labeled water to the water jar.
10. Return the nails from the paper towel labeled sand to the sand jar.

Day 3–5:

11. Obtain the mass of each group of nails (repeat steps 5–10) each day for five days. Record any changes you see in the nails for five days.

Data:

Day	Nails in Water		Nails in Sand	
	Mass	Observations	Mass	Observations
1				
2				
3				
4				
5				

TAKING IT FURTHER   While it might be very interesting to determine what factors cause things to rust, it might be even more valuable to know how to prevent rust. *What kind of paint best protects iron from rusting in water? How can you tell if color makes a difference?* You can test these ideas by coating nails with different substances and placing them in separate, identical jars of water. *Why do car manufacturers recommend waxing cars? Does it have to do with rust?* You could obtain several car pieces that were identical, apply wax to one group and no wax to the other group of pieces. Then use a spray bottle to spray the samples with water several times a day. To get results faster, a more corrosive (acidic) substance, such as vinegar, could be used.

In what ways do certain environmental conditions cause iron to rust faster? In areas that get snow and ice in the winter, salt is put on the streets. Some people claim that cars rust faster because of it. Also, ocean water, which contains salt and other substances, might also cause iron to rust faster, which means that individuals in coastal areas might experience more rusting. How can you prove that salt water causes iron to rust faster?

How can the presence of rust be beneficial? The topic of iron and ocean water is interesting because some scientists believe that burning fossil fuels is resulting in higher carbon dioxide levels, which increases the greenhouse effect of the Earth's atmosphere. The ocean is a huge sink for carbon dioxide. Iron is one of the substances that phytoplankton (little tiny animals that live in the ocean) need so adding additional iron to water in the form of rust may increase their numbers. Thereby, the phytoplankton may be able to be encouraged to use more carbon dioxide. There is also some evidence that bacteria (such as that found in sea water, where sunken ships rust) impacts rust rate. You may consider adding an antibacterial agent to water to see if it slows the rust rate.

Find the Secret Formula

Physical Science

BACKGROUND

Color-coated candies are very popular. Candy-coating is used for a number of reasons. Its hard, outer shell protects the soft candy- or gum-filling inside, plus a colorful candy shell makes the candy bright and appealing. While a bright green candy might be appealing, in many cases, a moss green or olive green candy would not be nearly as appetizing! Candy companies use scientists to help them formulate the colors for these candy coatings. The science of color-mixing is called chromatography, and there are many different chromatography techniques that scientists use.

Scientists can use chromatography to determine what colors are mixed in a substance (and sometimes the ingredients, too) based on the absorption differences among the components of the mixture. Simply put, because colors fall at different places on the spectrum, it is possible to separate one color into the colors that make it up. Paper chromatography involves using porous paper and capillary action to divide out the mixture. Since the fastest molecules will travel the greatest distance, the relative distance the molecules travel can be used to determine the rate of flow or the *Rf* value according to the equation shown:

$$Rf = \frac{\text{Distance the solute traveled}}{\text{Distance the solvent traveled}}$$

QUESTION

In what ways is the dye used in different candies that have the same color the same?

RESEARCH TOPICS

Chromatography, food additives, forensics

HYPOTHESIS

If the dyes in green M & M's® and a green Skittles® are divided into their component colors using chromatography, the Rf values will be identical. (The colors will travel the same distance up a piece of filter paper.)

MATERIALS

Goggles, chromatography paper (or round paper coffee filters), green Skittles® candies, green M & M's® candies, pencil, metric ruler, eyedropper, 2 identical jars (at least 14 cm tall), rubbing alcohol, transparent tape, paper towels, plastic wrap

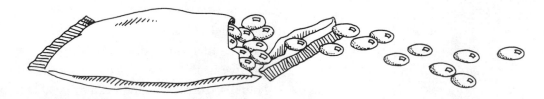

Skittles® and M & M's® are registered trademarks of Mars, Inc.

PROCEDURE

1. Cut 10 rectangles that are 14 cm long and 4 cm wide from 10 coffee filters. Prepare five filter paper strips for each brand of candy.
2. Use a pencil and metric ruler to draw a straight line exactly 2 cm up on the 4 cm side of each filter.
3. Look at the ingredients on each candy package and record the dye used. Place the candy piece to be tested in a small dish. Place four drops of water slowly on the piece of candy to dissolve the outside layer.
4. Place some of the green solution in an eyedropper. Place one drop of the solution in the center of the 2 cm line on the coffee filter and allow to dry. (To make the colors darker, add another drop of colored water to the same spot and allow the paper to dry between additions.) Prepare five strips for the first brand of candy.
5. Repeat steps 3 and 4 for the second brand of candy.
6. Put 5 mL of rubbing alcohol in the bottom of the jar. Use small pieces of tape (1 cm square) to place the five filter strips for the first brand of candy in the jar so that the bottom of the 4 cm marked sides, not the spots of green dye, are touching the alcohol. Label the jar with the name of the first brand of candy.
7. Repeat step 6 for the second brand of candy.
8. Leave the filters in the alcohol for exactly 15 minutes. Remove the paper filters and lay them flat on a paper towel to dry.
9. Measure the distance the color moved and record on the data table.

Hint: The solute is the color from the candy and the solvent is the alcohol. Experiment with using different types of candy. It may be possible to use water rather than alcohol to separate the color dyes since most candy coatings are water soluble.

TAKING IT FURTHER

Though the dye used in food is often listed on the package, the same dye may also be used in nonfood items such as latex paints and water-soluble markers. Find out if the dyes can be separated. For permanent ink markers, use nail polisher remover as the solvent.

The dye in fruit-flavored powdered drinks and other drink mixes can be divided out using chromatography. Just add a little water to each powder and follow the same procedure using water instead of alcohol as the solvent. Green drink mixes will often divide into beautiful bands of blue and yellow. Try purple drink mixes, too.

It would also be interesting to compare the pigments in natural foods to artificial dyes to see if they contain similar substances.

Getting Wet, Staying Warm

Physical Science

BACKGROUND

Have you ever been outside when it is really cold? When you are sledding, camping, or doing other activities, you better dress correctly. Human beings that do not dress correctly for cold temperatures are at risk for hypothermia and frostbite. Generally, it is advised that an individual put several layers of clothing on during cold weather. If the person gets too warm, the layers can be removed one at a time. It is best if the layers are shed before the clothing beneath becomes damp. Cotton is not the best insulator because if it becomes wet, it dries slowly and actually conducts heat away from the human body.

QUESTION

What type of material would provide the best insulation for the human body when wet?

RESEARCH TOPICS

Clothing materials (such as cotton and wool), insulation

HYPOTHESIS

If two pieces of wool and cotton are soaked in water, the wool will prevent heat loss better than the cotton.

MATERIALS

Two jars (approximately 400 mL capacity) with lids, hot water, two alcohol thermometers, a piece of wool and a piece of cotton material cut into 24 cm x 24 cm squares, two rubber bands

PROCEDURE

1. Cut a piece of wool and a piece of cotton so that they will fit completely around the jar (24 cm x 24 cm).
2. Place a thermometer inside each jar. Fill the two jars with hot water.
3. Take an initial temperature reading in one jar. Replace the lid.
4. Wrap one jar in the cotton material. Gather the extra material at the top of the jar and fasten with a rubber band. The thermometer should stick out the top so that it can be removed to take readings.
5. Take an initial temperature reading in the second jar. Replace the lid.
6. Wrap one jar in the wool material. Gather the extra material at the top of the jar and fasten with a rubber band. The thermometer should stick out the top so that it can be removed to take readings.
7. After 10 minutes, remove the thermometer from the cotton jar and take a reading. Then unwrap the wool jar and take a reading. Record the temperatures on the data table.
8. Repeat step 7 until three identical temperature readings are obtained in each jar.

Data:

Temperatures

Time (Minutes)	Cotton	Wool
0 minutes		
10 minutes		
20 minutes		
30 minutes		
40 minutes		
50 minutes		

Hints: The jars must be placed in the same area so that they have the same surrounding temperature. Since human beings are mostly water, water is a good substance to use for this experiment.

TAKING IT FURTHER

How much more effective are manufactured materials than natural fibers as insulators? There are many new fabric blends (Gortex, polypropylene) that are made of manufactured material and claim to have a better insulating capacity than natural fibers. These claims can easily be tested using the same procedure on the previous page. Various combinations of fabrics can also be tested to see if the insulating ability can be improved.

NASA has discovered a new solid called aerogel that is very lightweight but has amazing insulating capacity. Find out what it is used for, see if you can get some, and compare it to more traditional insulation methods.

What type of insulation material keeps your home the warmest? There are also many different brands of home insulators. It would be interesting to test some of these brands and then do a price comparison. Compare the effectiveness of some of the insulators to wadded up newspaper.

What is the best way to insulate windows? Window insulation has been studied as long as windows have been around. Use different techniques to insulate a window and determine a method to show which is the best way to insulate windows.

Hot Food, Coming Through!

Physical Science

BACKGROUND

As the name implies, a microwave oven uses microwaves (roughly 2,500 megahertz) to heat food. Fats, sugars, and water in the food absorb the microwave energy and convert it to atomic motion—heat (which we detect as a change in temperature). The penetration of the microwaves is generally fairly even throughout the food but thicker foods may be harder to penetrate and conversely, thinner foods are easier to penetrate. This wave interference results in hot and cold areas in food. In contrast, a conventional oven uses conduction to heat the interior of foods. To heat food by conduction, there must be direct contact with the heat source (they must be touching).

QUESTION

How quickly does water cooked in a microwave oven cool off faster than water that is cooked in a gas oven?

RESEARCH TOPICS

Microwave ovens, microwave, temperature, heat, heat transfer (conduction, convection, radiation)

HYPOTHESIS

If water is heated in a microwave and in a conventional gas oven to a temperature of 80 degrees Celsius, the water heated in the microwave will cool by 30 degrees in less time than the water heated in the gas oven.

MATERIALS

Microwave oven, gas oven (electric oven can be substituted), water (or food item to be tested), two identical heat resistant (cookware) bowls or coffee mugs, two alcohol thermometers

PROCEDURE

1. Pour equal amounts of cold water into identical coffee mugs or cookware. Experiment with the amount of time needed for the microwave to heat the water to 80°C.
2. Heat the water in the gas oven (electric oven) to 80°C.
3. Remove both the bowl from the microwave oven and the bowl from the gas oven at the same time. Record the temperature of the water in each bowl. Read and record the temperature in each bowl every minute until the water heated in the microwave oven has cooled to 50°C.

CAUTION: CONDUCT THIS EXPERIMENT WITH ADULT SUPERVISION. BE SURE THE COOKWARE CAN BE USED IN THE MICROWAVE AND IN A GAS OR ELECTRIC OVEN.

Data:

Time	Microwave Oven	Gas Oven
Initial Reading		
1 minute		
2 minutes		
3 minutes		
4 minutes		
5 minutes		

Hints: The water can be heated to boiling but extreme care must be taken to avoid injury. *Caution: The water heated in the microwave may erupt into a boil as the container is moved after being heated.* The data for this experiment will result in a line graph that has two lines, one for the microwave heat loss and one for the gas oven heat loss.

TAKING IT FURTHER *How much faster does food heated in a microwave cool compare with food heated in a gas oven (electric oven)?* Try heating your favorite food in both types of ovens and determine how fast the food cools. If the food does cool faster, it may be that only certain types of food lose heat quickly, such as foods that have high water content or very high sugar content. If there is a difference, use the research to find the explanation. For another test, heat food in a microwave oven and compare how much faster it cools with food heated on a stove top (hot plate). Read the labels on your equipment to be sure the cookware is suitable for both heat sources.

You might also want to determine if the microwave oven changes the taste or texture of food in any way. Try to think of some quality about the food that might change as a result of the fast cooking in the microwave, then test for that quality.

Magnetic Attraction

BACKGROUND The Earth has a magnetic field. Many animals seem to use the magnetic field in various ways, such as finding direction for migration. Magnetite, a magnetic mineral also called lodestone, was used by ancient healers hundreds of years ago. The interest in magnets has been rekindled recently and some individuals suggest that the energy field of magnets may affect pain receptors and reduce the pain intensity messages sent to the human brain. Other studies have shown no difference in pain intensity reports by subjects who wear magnets and those who do not. It might be interesting to study how magnets impact a variety of living organisms.

QUESTION What affect do magnets have on crickets?

RESEARCH TOPICS Arthropod, cricket, magnets, magnets

HYPOTHESIS If magnets are placed below a cricket colony, the health of the colony will be improved as demonstrated by an increased number of offspring.

MATERIALS 24 crickets, two 10-gallon (45.46 L) aquariums with lids, potting soil, dead leaves, sticks, and other ground cover, oatmeal, top of plastic water bottles, eyedropper, 12 magnets, potatoes and other food scraps (such as dry dog food, spinach, oats), small jar (approximately 200 mL volume), spray bottle

PROCEDURE
1. Place potting soil in the aquariums to a depth of 10 cm. Place leaf litter, dried weeds, sticks and other debris on top of the soil so that the same amount of each substance is in the same area in each aquarium.
2. Place a small amount of food scraps in each aquarium. (The same amount of food should be placed in the same area in each aquarium.)
3. Use the lids of 2-liter bottles as water dishes. Place one lid filled with water in each of the aquariums. Fill the small jar with water. Pour the water into the spray bottle. Spray the same amount of water in approximately the same areas in each aquarium. (To be sure that the amount of water is the same, empty the spray bottle into the first aquarium and then refill it to spray the second aquarium. The soil should be moist but not soaked.)
4. Obtain 12 small magnets and place them under the first aquarium at approximately equal distance from

each other. Record the size and strength of the magnets. (This information should be located on the package in which the magnets were purchased.)

5. Obtain 24 crickets (either captured outside or purchased from a pet store). Determine both the common name and the scientific name of the crickets used and record the information in your science journal.

6. Place 12 crickets in each aquarium and then cover it with the lid.

7. Each week, add fresh food and water to each aquarium in equal amounts to sustain the crickets. Food and water should be plentiful so that these are not population limiting factors. Observe the behavior of the crickets in each aquarium at the same time each day for about 15 minutes. Record the observations in your informal journal.

Hints: If crickets are not available, mealworms are another organism that can be studied. When you set up the experiment with two jars, make sure that everything is exactly the same. Two types of mealworms are sold in bait shops and pet stores, regular and jumbo. The jumbo does not have as fast a life cycle. Part of a potato or apple will probably provide the necessary water but if the beetles appear to require more, place a damp paper towel on top of the grain layers. The paper towel can be dampened by adding small amounts of water with an eyedropper.

Mealworms undergo a complete metamorphosis, changing from an egg, to a larva, to a pupa, and finally to a beetle. The adult beetles have an exoskeleton; a hard outer covering that protects and supports the insects bodies. You may also want to measure the length and width of the adult bodies to see if there is a size difference as a result of the differential treatment.

TAKING IT FURTHER *How are plants affected by an electromagnetic field?* Try raising a plant in the field of an electromagnet and see if there are any changes. As data, the leaves could be counted and leaf surfaces measured. The root of each plant should also be scrutinized at the end of the experiment.

More Harm Than Good?

Life Science

BACKGROUND

In nature, when plants die the material is recycled by the soil and becomes the nutrients for the next generation. When human beings plant crops and then harvest them, the nutrients are removed from the soil. Over time, the soil may become depleted of nutrients necessary for the survival of the crop. To prevent soil depletion, a farmer might leave some plant materials on the field or rotate crops that have different nutrient needs.

In most areas, however, some fertilizer is usually added to increase the health of plants by adding necessary nutrients. The organisms that live in soil are often beneficial to the crops grown there. Earthworms, for example, keep the soil aerated and help breakdown organic material. When fertilizer is added to the soil, it impacts everything in the soil—for good or bad.

QUESTION

What affect does fertilizer have on the health of earthworms that live in the soil?

RESEARCH TOPICS

Earthworms, fertilizer, nitrogen, soil

HYPOTHESIS

If a chemical plant food is mixed according to label directions and added to soil, the health of worms will be negatively impacted as demonstrated by a decrease in the total mass of the worms.

MATERIALS

12 worms, fertilizer (include brand name), distilled water, potting soil, organic matter (leaves, orange peel, banana peel, apple pieces, bread), two 2-liter plastic bottles, scissors, tape, balance, pushpin, duct tape, black construction paper

PROCEDURE

1. Use two 2-liter plastic bottles from the same type of drink and rinse thoroughly. Use the pushpin to make four holes in the spout end of each bottle. Cut the top off the bottles to 10 cm below the spout. Save the lids and the tops of the bottles. Use a pushpin to place small holes in the bottoms to allow drainage.
2. In the bottom of each bottle, place 400 mL of potting soil. Gather equal amounts of organic matter such as banana peels, orange peels, and leaves (no animal products such as meat or eggs). Then place equal amounts of organic matter on top of the potting soil. Add potting soil to the bottles in equal amounts until the bottles are filled to 4 cm from the top.
3. Obtain 12 worms and rinse off the dirt. Record the common and scientific name of the worms in your informal journal.

4. Prepare the fertilizer according to label instructions. Mark one bottle "experimental" and pour 200 mL of the fertilizer solution into the bottle. Add 200 mL of distilled water to the other bottle.

5. Divide the worms into equal piles with six worms each. Use the balance to obtain the mass of each set of worms. Place the earthworms on a paper towel or in a small container. *If the worms are placed in a container, remember to subtract the mass of the dish from the total mass to find out the mass of the worms.*

6. Place one group of worms into the bottle to which you have added fertilizer. Record the initial mass on the data table. Repeat for the control bottle. Tape the tops back on the bottles using duct tape. The same amount of tape must be applied to the same areas on both bottles. Make a construction paper sleeve to cover each bottle.

7. The experiment should run for about two months. At the end of each week, remove the worms, rinse them, find out their mass, and then put them back into the same bottle. Add organic matter and water to the soil as needed to keep the soil moist but not soaked. Remember to add the same amount of everything to each bottle except the fertilizer solution. Record your observations in your informal journal.

Hints: Allergies and asthma may be triggered by the decaying matter or by the odor of the soil so do not try this experiment if you have had problems in the past. The worms can climb out of the bottles if the tops are not taped securely. Additionally, the tops and lids help the systems retain moisture. Plants may also be grown on top of the soil but be sure to include the species and genus as well as the planting method in the procedure.

TAKING IT FURTHER   *If a little fertilizer is good, is more better?* Try making fertilizer to regular strength and then twice the strength to see if adding more fertilizer is good or bad for the worms in the soil.

What impact do other chemicals placed on plants have on worms? Weed killers and pesticides are put on plants but those chemicals wash into the soil where they come into contact with worms.

"Eggshellent" Absorption

Life Science

BACKGROUND

If you spend a lot of time in water in a bathtub or swimming area, your skin's natural oil (called sebum) is washed away and your skin will begin to absorb water. (Fingernails and toenails also absorb some water, which causes them to become soft.)

Diffusion involves the movement of molecules from a place where there are a lot of molecules, to where there are fewer molecules. Osmosis is the same thing except that a cell membrane is involved. Fluids move into and out of a cell until there is a balance. If you put cells in water, the water will move into the cells. If you put cells in a sugary substance, the water will move out of the cell. When you climb into a bathtub, there is more water outside the cells than inside so water will move into your cells by osmosis. Your skin does take on water. So why the raisin look? Your skin has small attachments and those attachments are pulling the skin down in some places and not others—this is kind of like the gathering of a skirt—but the bunching up of skin occurs because the skin is thicker on the fingers and toes than on the other places on the body.

QUESTION

Why does my skin get pruny in water?

RESEARCH TOPICS

Osmosis, diffusion, epidermis, cell membrane, semipermeable

HYPOTHESIS

An egg placed in light corn syrup will lose mass while an identical egg placed in distilled water will gain mass.

MATERIALS

Two chicken eggs, white vinegar, light corn syrup, two identical jars with a capacity of 250 mL, balance

PROCEDURE

Day 1:
1. Place one chicken egg in each jar. Add 200 mL of vinegar to each jar. (The egg should be completely submerged. If the egg is not submerged, add more vinegar but keep track of the exact volume used and use that volume throughout the experiment.)

Day 2:
2. Remove the eggs from the vinegar and observe them. The hard shell should be completely removed, leaving a rubbery-type membrane. Place each egg in 200 mL of distilled water for two hours.
3. Remove the eggs from the water. Rinse both jars thoroughly. To the control jar, add 200 mL of distilled water. Label the jar.

4. In the experimental jar, add 200 mL of light corn syrup. Label the jar.
5. Obtain the mass of both eggs. Place one egg in the distilled water and one egg in the corn syrup.

Day 3:
6. Remove the eggs from the solutions. Use the balance to find out the mass of each egg.

Hints: The outer membrane of the egg represents human skin. In the display, there are many ways to demonstrate diffusion:

- Place one drop of food coloring in a beaker that is filled with water. The dye is very concentrated in one area at first but eventually will spread throughout the liquid by diffusion.
- Place safe substances with strong odors (such as cinnamon) inside balloons. Have participants try to identify the substance in the balloon by smelling the outside. The odors are able to move out through small pores in the balloon.
- Pour salt into a beaker of water until no more will dissolve and the salt starts to come out of solution and settle to the bottom; the solution will be saturated (it has as much salt as it can hold). In another beaker, have an equal amount of distilled water. Place one large, raw french fry into each beaker. The two french fries should be approximately the same size. The french fry in the beaker with the salt will shrivel, while the french fry in the beaker of water becomes very firm and crisp. In the salt water, there was more stuff outside the cells so the water moved out of the cell to the surroundings, which is what causes the squishy look. In the water, there was more stuff inside the cell so the water moved from the outside to the inside making the potato appear firm. The mass of the potato slices can be obtained before and after being placed in the solutions as a way to quantify the data.
- The membrane of human cells is semipermeable. It allows certain molecules to pass through. Place about 500 grams of salt in a colander with bean seeds or polystyrene foam balls with a diameter of at least 2 cm. The salt can move freely through the holes. The cell membrane has small holes similar to the colander. Some molecules can pass through the membrane freely, others need assistance to move through the cell, and some molecules cannot move into the cell at all.
- An orange has a protective outer covering that consists of more than one layer. The epidermis of the orange protects the tender inside similar to the way skin protects humans.

TAKING IT FURTHER

For certain injuries, a bath in healing salts might be recommended. Compare the prune look caused by healing salts with the look caused by plain water.

Commercial bubble baths and bath oils may also cause a difference in the pruny effect. Test several brands to see what the differences are. Compare the ingredients for each thing you test. Can you figure out what ingredient (if any) may change the effect?

Soil Survivors

BACKGROUND

During winter in some areas, few if any insects are seen in the frigid environment but when the Earth begins to awaken from its winter sedateness, suddenly buzzing and crawling insects appear everywhere. Where do they come from? While many insects don't survive the cold temperatures of winter, others have evolved with some very clever survival techniques. Cluster flies hide in warm areas, such as homes. Some species of mosquitoes look for dark, damp places, such as a basement to hibernate, while others lay eggs, the adults die off, and the eggs hatch when conditions are better. Some arthropods migrate, such as locusts, bees, wasps, and monarchs.

QUESTION

How do insects survive in winter when the ground remains frozen for months?

RESEARCH TOPICS

Hibernation, dormancy, arthropods, insects

HYPOTHESIS

If frozen soil is brought in from outside and kept warm and moist, insects will appear.

MATERIALS

Two 2-liter bottles, 1 liter of potting soil, 1 liter of frozen soil from a garden or yard area, plastic wrap, rubber bands, spray bottles, water, scissors, magnifying glass or hand lens

PROCEDURE

1. Cut the spout end off each 2-liter bottle. Place 1 liter of potting soil in one bottle and 1 liter of frozen soil from a yard in the other. Look carefully at each soil sample to determine if there are any animals already present in the soil.
2. Add the same amount of water to each bottle.
3. Cut two pieces of plastic wrap the exact same size. Use a rubber band to seal the plastic wrap securely to the top of each bottle.
4. Keep the bottles warm (26° C or about room temperature) and keep the soil moist but not soaked. Each day, record the number of organisms of each different species that appear in the soil. Continue your observations for as many days as possible.

Data:

Day	Number of Individuals		
	Species 1	Species 2	Species 3
1			
2			
3			
4			
5			

Hints: The soil should come from an area of the yard or garden where multiple insects are visible during warm weather (such as under a drainage spout or near the foundation). No critters should emerge in the potting soil because it should have been sterilized prior to being sold.

TAKING IT FURTHER

How can you prevent insects from infesting and hatching in food? It is really amazing how many insects share our world. People often do not realize that we regularly consume insects and their parts whether or not we mean to. For example, take different brands of grains (flour, cornmeal, oatmeal, bran) and place them in a warm moist area. A spray bottle can be used to keep them moist if desired. Be sure to keep each container covered because you will be amazed at what emerges. What do you think you will see, and how do you think it got there?

Check with the local Extension Office in your area or locate an entomologist and find out what types of infestations are likely in food products. Boxed breakfast cereals are another source of insects and insect parts. Use a magnifying glass to check the crumbs at the bottom of the box. Leave some of the cereal in a warm, moist place (in a sealed container with some air holes) and see if anything crawls out.

Rodent food is another possible breeding place for small arthropods. Just place a small amount of seed food in a warm, moist area. People who own rodents should be sure to keep the food dry and cool to avoid finding crawling critters in their home.

Is Soil Good for Plants?

Earth & Space Science

BACKGROUND While there are many types of soils, soil textures can be divided into three categories according to particle size: sandy soils, clay soils, and loam soils. The sizes and amounts of the mineral particles present in the soil determine some characteristics. While sandy soil has good drainage and good aeration, it tends not to store water well. Clay holds water but does not drain well. Loam soil has a more even mixture of particle sizes that allows it to hold both air and water well while providing adequate drainage.

QUESTION What type of soil is best for plants?

RESEARCH TOPICS Soil science, soil nutrients, soil profile, soil formation, soil types (silt, loam, sand, clay), soil management

HYPOTHESIS If grass (include both common and scientific name) is grown in clay soil and loam soil, the grass in the loam soil will grow taller.

MATERIALS 20 empty, 35-mm film canisters, grass seed, clay soil, loam soil, water, pushpin, graduated cylinder, metric ruler

PROCEDURE
1. Use the pushpin to make five holes in the bottom of each film canister. Be sure the holes are in the same location on each canister.
2. Determine the amount of soil necessary to fill 10 of the canisters three-fourths full with clay soil.
3. Add the same amount of loam soil to the other 10 canisters.
4. Follow the directions on the seed packet to plant two seeds in each film canister.
5. Add the desired amount of water so that each canister receives the same amount.
6. Record observations each day. For the first five days, count the number of seeds that germinated in each canister.
7. After the seeds germinate, measure the height of each seed in a single canister and then divide by the number of seeds in the canister to obtain the average height of the plants in each canister.

Data:

	Number of Seeds Germinated			Average Height of Seedlings	
	Clay Soil	Loam Soil		Clay Soil	Loam Soil
1					
2					
3					
4					
5					

Hints: The film canisters can be obtained from any store that processes film. A method for drainage will have to be devised, such as placing the canisters on a screen to allow excess water to run through them.

TAKING IT FURTHER

Many different types of soils can be studied. Various plants have different soil type requirements.

Try planting native (local) plants in soil you dig up from your yard and in other types of soil that are not native to your area. For example, if you live in the Midwest, see if you can get red clay soil from the South and sandy soil from a coast or desert. Which soil is better for your plants? Is there a significant difference? Be sure to research the areas in which the local plant you choose is also found.

Leaves Up, Roots Down

Earth & Space Science

BACKGROUND   If you saw a big, mean dog growling, your first instinct would be to get to a safe place. In that example, the dog is a stimulus and your leaving the area is the response. All living things respond to certain stimuli. Plants cannot pull up their roots and run from a dog, but they do respond to a stimulus, such as the sun. Tropism is the growth of a plant in a definite direction in response to a stimulus. In positive tropism, the plant grows toward the stimulus and in negative tropism the plant grows away from the stimulus. In phototropism, a plant moves toward the light while in gravitropism the plant grows in response to gravity. While the roots of a plant are positively gravitropic (the roots grow down deeper into the soil), the shoot of the plant is negatively gravitropic (meaning it grows up).

QUESTION   In what directions do roots and plant shoots grow if the positions of seeds and plants are changed?

RESEARCH TOPICS   Tropism, phototropism, gravitropism, photosynthesis

HYPOTHESIS   If one sunflower seed is planted with the tip down and another with the tip up, the roots of both seeds will grow down.

MATERIALS   Clear glass jar, potting soil, water, sunflower seeds, ruler

PROCEDURE
1. Fill the jar with potting soil.
2. Place two seeds in the jar on opposite sides.
3. Use your index fingers to push both seeds below the soil at the same time for the same distance. Label the outside of the jar so that the seeds can be identified. (For example, use the labels "Seed 1" and "Seed 2.") Place the jar in a dark area.
4. Moisten the soil and keep the soil moist.
5. Make daily observations. Measure the length of the root and the sprout of each plant each day.

Data:

Day	Lengths				Day	Lengths			
	Root 1	Root 2	Sprout 1	Sprout 2		Root 1	Root 2	Sprout 1	Sprout 2
1					6				
2					7				
3					8				
4					9				
5					10				

Hints: The seeds should be from the same packet which will control for prior treatment. Any seed can be used that has an obvious top and bottom. The seeds could also be grown in a clear plastic sandwich bag with a moist paper towel.

TAKING IT FURTHER Multiple experiments with plants are possible. After the shoot and root begin to grow, for example, the jar could simply be inverted to see if the root and shoot will change direction.

Using a milk carton, create a maze so that the shoot has to follow a complicated trail in order to get to the sun. Build several identical mazes, and test several different plants to see which kind is best-equipped to get to the sun. Does that plant need more sun than the others to do well?

Crop Circles

Earth & Space Science

BACKGROUND

Have you ever purchased potting soil? Isn't it amazing that someone can put dirt in a bag and sell it? Why are people willing to pay money for soil when there is so much soil in the world? Apparently, some soils must be better than others. People usually cannot do too much about the type of soil found in their yard, but if the characteristics of good soil can be determined for a certain type of plant (say, the type of grass your parents like to grow in the yard), maybe you could figure out a way to add something to the surface of soil to make it better. Most living things need pretty much the same basic things you do: water, food, air, space, and sunlight. While soil is generally considered a renewable resource, it can take hundreds of years for depleted soil to become rich again. Soil becomes depleted when the average rate of topsoil erosion exceeds the rate at which the topsoil is replaced. Erosion is the removal and transport of earth materials by natural agents such as water (running water, rain, snow, ocean waves, precipitation, glaciation) and wind. While topsoil is replaced at only a few centimeters every thousand years or so, topsoil can be depleted by several centimeters in a decade, which results in soil depletion.

QUESTION

What is the best way to plant crops to avoid soil erosion?

RESEARCH TOPICS

Erosion, contour farming, crop research

HYPOTHESIS

If crops are planted so that the rows run perpendicular to the hill, there will be less soil erosion.

MATERIALS

Two plastic shoe boxes, 4 liters of soil, mullet seed (or any plant seed that germinates quickly), plastic knife, ruler, box cutter, two books about 6 cm thick, spray bottle, water, container to catch runoff

PROCEDURE

1. Place equal amounts of soil in each box and pack the soil down slightly with the palm of your hand.
2. WITH ADULT SUPERVISION: Use the box cutter to place a large slit on one of the short sides of each rectangular shoe box that is 1 cm in width and just above the soil line. The slits must be the same size in each box.
3. Use the knife to cut furrows in the soil of one box in rows that are 4 cm apart and run vertically to the long side. Place seeds every centimeter in the rows and cover with about 2 mm of soil.
4. Use the knife to cut furrows in the soil of the second box that run vertically to the short side of the box and are 4 cm apart. Place seeds every centimeter in the rows and cover with about 2 mm of soil.

5. Allow the plants to germinate and grow to a height of 2 cm. Cut the crop to the same height in both boxes.
6. Use the books to prop the short end of each shoe box up so that all the water will run down toward the slit in the other short side. Place a container at the slit of each box to catch the runoff.
7. Spray water quickly over the top of the soil to simulate a downpour of rain about every five days.
8. Allow the runoff to settle. (This is the fluid material that spilled out of the slit of the boxes.) Then, pour off the excess water. Allow the solid material to dry before finding out the mass of the soil lost in each box each time there is a downpour.

Data:

Week	Mass of Soil	
	Horizontal Rows	Vertical Rows
1		
2		
3		
4		
5		

Hints: Mullet seeds are sold as parakeet food in pet stores. This seed is inexpensive, available, and quick to germinate but any available crop seed can be planted as long as the same seeds are planted in each box. The best way to set up this experiment would be to create a miniature soil profile and place darker soil on top so that the color of the soil loss could also be compared to show that the valuable top soil is what is lost.

TAKING IT FURTHER You can study many different types of soils in your area. To identify soil types, you may need to find a professional in your area that can help. To do this, talk to the teachers at your school, or contact the local university or Department of Natural Resources local office. Soil is so important that every area has a map that identifies the soil type in certain areas. The color and consistency of soil varies greatly in different areas: in the great salt flats of Utah some soil is white in color, in Oklahoma the soil is often brick red, in Arizona some soils look pink, and in Nebraska the soil tends to be tan to black. When farmers add pesticides and fertilizers to their crops but have erosion problems, those chemicals can be washed directly into the streams in the area. One way to show this would be to add sodium chloride to soil and then spray enough water to generate runoff that can be collected. Use a dilute solution of silver nitrate to test for chlorine in the water you collected. If the solution turns milky white, chlorine is present in the water that passed through the soil, which would indicate that any other chemicals that the farmer added would also wash into the streams. (Talk to your teacher about using this test. Silver nitrate solution [1M] can be made by dissolving 169.89 g of silver nitrate in 1 liter of distilled water.)

Can Elodea Cope with Soap?

BACKGROUND

Do you like to go camping in a tent? When people camp, they sometimes use soaps and detergents to wash both their dishes and their bodies. Some people will wash their dishes near a lake and the soap travels with the water into the lake. Though many people do care about the environment, they can accidentally do things that harm nature's delicate balance. Soap is something people use every day, and many campers neither realize that the soaps used are damaging nor that there are biodegradable alternatives.

QUESTION

How does a nonbiodegradable dish detergent affect aquatic plants?

RESEARCH TOPICS

Biodegradable, phosphates, water pollution, detergent, aquatic plants

HYPOTHESIS

If nonbiodegradable dish detergent is added to water, it will have a negative effect on the health of elodea.

MATERIALS

Two sterilized jars that are exactly the same size, dechlorinated water, sprigs of elodea, nonbiodegradable dish detergent

PROCEDURE

1. Place equal amounts of dechlorinated water in the jars.
2. Count the leaves on the sprigs of the elodea and divide the sprigs into two equal groups. Add the elodea to the jars.
3. Add one drop of liquid dish soap to one of the jars. Label the jar.
4. Record observations daily and count the number of leaves that remain on each sprig.

Data:

Day	Number of Leaves		Observations	
	Experimental	Control	Experimental	Control
1				
2				
3				
4				
5				
6				
7				
8				

Hints: Any aquatic plant available in your area can be studied, but the results can only be applied to the brand of detergent and the species of plant you used. This experiment is interesting for campers because it is not unusual for people to wash dishes near a lake using soap that can be harmful.

TAKING IT FURTHER   There are many products used by people that find their way into natural environments. It can be interesting to study the impact those products have on members of an ecosystem. For example, an individual may not consider the impact that nonbiodegradable shampoo might have on the environment when using it in a wilderness area. Another substance to explore would be sunscreen lotion which is frequently washed off with hand soap near a lake or stream. Both substances are washed into the body of water.

Backpackers must travel light and so often use dirt or gravel to rub any food out of their dishes and then use a small amount of biodegradable soap to wash them. Try to find the best way for campers to clean equipment without damaging the ecosystem.

Acid Rain, Oh, What a Pain!

Earth & Space Science

BACKGROUND

All rain is acidic and has always been. Natural rain has a pH around 5.6. Precipitation becomes acidic from natural causes such as volcanic eruptions and animals breathing. When human beings burn coal to generate electricity, however, large amounts of sulfur are introduced into the atmosphere which combine with rain to form sulfuric acid. Nitrogen and carbon compounds combine with water to form nitric acid and carbonic acid. Acid precipitation can destroy living things and it can also destroy structures that human beings have created, such as statues and monuments.

QUESTION

How does "acid" rain affect structures made by humans?

RESEARCH TOPICS

Acid rain, pH scale, acidity, alkalinity, air pollution

HYPOTHESIS

If a marble statue is exposed to rain with a pH of 5, it will lose mass and change in appearance.

MATERIALS

Goggles, two marble slabs (sometimes marble can be obtained free from companies that produce monuments but landscaping stores also sell marble chips), white vinegar, balance, pH paper, distilled water, graduated cylinder, two identical sterilized jars, tongs, paper towels

PROCEDURE

1. Put on your goggles. Obtain 500 mL of distilled water. Add 150 mL of white vinegar. Check the pH of the solution. If a pH of 5 is not obtained, continue to add white vinegar.
2. Measure the amount of acidic solution. Pour the solution into one jar. Pour an equal amount of distilled water into another jar.
3. Find out the mass of each marble sample. Record your observations about the marble.
4. Using tongs, carefully place one piece of marble in each of the jars. The marble should be completely below the surface of the fluid.
5. Place the jars in the same area. Determine the mass of the marble in each jar separately at a predetermined time each day.

Data:

Day	Mass of Marble		Observations	
	In Water	In Vinegar	Marble in Water	Marble in Vinegar
1				
2				
3				
4				
5				
6				
7				
8				

Hints: To simulate a rainshower more accurately, pour the solutions in spray bottles and squirt the marble pieces each day.

TAKING IT FURTHER *What impact does "acid" rain have on elodea (a water plant)? Obtain sprigs of elodea. Place one in fluid with a reduced pH and one in water only. Count the number of leaves daily for data.*

How does limestone affect the pH of rainwater and lake water? If human activities are lowering the pH of rain, that could impact many other species. In areas where there is a lot of limestone, there are fewer cases of episodic acidification, which happens where precipitation with a low pH drastically changes the pH of a lake and results in massive fish kills. Could it be that the limestone acts as a buffer to neutralize the acid? Conduct an experiment where limestone is added to soil in one container and not the other. Check to see if the pH of the runoff changes.

Acid Reign

BACKGROUND

Have you ever seen a commercial for a fabric softener that says something like, "Makes clothes smell as fresh as the air after a spring rain shower"? The air does smell different after it rains—fresh and clean. That is partly because rain does clean some of the chemicals and dirt out of air. Rain is good for air, but is air good for the rain? While unpolluted rainwater has a pH of about 5.6, the pH of rain can be lowered by chemicals in the atmosphere such as carbon dioxide, nitrogen, and sulfur containing compounds which combine with the water to produce carbonic acid, nitric acid, and sulfuric acid respectively. The acids then fall with the rain which can have a pH as low as 1.5.

QUESTION

How does the pH of precipitation change when it rains for a long time?

RESEARCH TOPICS

Acid rain, hydrologic cycle, pH scale, acidic, basic, air pollution

HYPOTHESIS

If the pH of precipitation is measured every 10 minutes as it is falling, the pH of the rain will increase.

MATERIALS

Narrow range pH paper (or a pH probe), clean cups

PROCEDURE

1. Wait for a rain- or snowstorm. (For safety reasons, do not go out in storms with high winds, hail, or thunder and lightning.) Set a cup in an area where you will catch the precipitation. Do not put the cup under a drainage spout or tree.
2. Bring the cup in after some precipitation has been collected and immediately test the pH. Only about 1 centimeter of water is necessary. Record the pH on the data table.
3. Repeat step 2 every 10 minutes until the precipitation stops.
4. Test the pH of rain during several storms and in other locations if possible.

Data:

Time (minutes)	ph Level
10	
20	
30	
40	
50	

Time (minutes)	ph Level
60	
70	
80	
90	
100	

Hints: It has been said that rain cleans the air. If that is true, then the pH of the rain should decrease over the length of time the precipitation is falling.

TAKING IT FURTHER

How does the pH of precipitation change throughout the year? Compare the pH of the precipitation during different times of the day or during different seasons of the year.

The pollution produced in one area does not always fall back on that area. Sometimes the wind carries pollution and it rains down over natural areas. You may be able to test the pH of the rain in natural areas that are in the path of the wind that blows through a city. Test the pH of the water in the area as well. If the water in the natural area has a pH lower than the rain, then there must be something in the soil or perhaps a ground water source that lowers the pH naturally.

In what way is the pH of lake water affected by precipitation? There is a phenomena called episodic acidification where precipitation with a low pH drastically changes the pH of a lake and results in massive fish kills. Test the pH of lake water before and after precipitation has fallen to see if the pH changes.

Decay Is Okay!

Earth & Space Science

BACKGROUND

Do the creatures that live in soil accelerate decay? (Maybe for an extension here, it would be a good idea to add something about whether or not it's true that one bad apple spoils the whole lot. Actually, it is true because one bad apple produces a substance that can cause the other apples to become rotten.) Some people think that it is best to add some old compost to speed up the decay of new compost. There is a balance in nature, and decay is part of that balance. The organisms that help to break down organic material and recycle nutrients are called decomposers. Approximately 20 percent of the material sent to landfills is compostable yard waste (tree clippings, leaves, grass, etc.) as well as other organic material such as food scraps. Plant material can be easily recycled by anyone who has a yard and turned into a valuable garden resource called compost. Compost not only adds nutrients to the soil, but it also improves soil texture and water-holding capacity.

QUESTION

How do the creatures that live in soil accelerate decay? (**Caution:** This activity should not be attempted by or near anyone with allergies, asthma, or breathing disorders.)

RESEARCH TOPICS

Compost, humus, decomposers, arthropods, earthworms, garbology, organic, inorganic

HYPOTHESIS

If soil is sterilized in the microwave, organic matter will take much longer to decay.

MATERIALS

Microwave, fertile soil from an outside area (potting soil will not work), an orange peel, a banana peel, a piece of bread, a balance, two jars the same size, glass plate, pushpin, tongs

PROCEDURE

1. Sterilize the jars. Measure and divide the soil equally into two piles. Record the exact amount of soil that will be placed in each jar.
2. Place half the soil on a glass plate and place the soil and plate in the microwave for 10 minutes. The microwaving should be done outside or in a well ventilated area. Allow the soil to cool to room temperature.
3. Obtain the mass of the two groups of orange peels, banana peels, and bread slices.
4. Pour 2 cm of soil in each jar. Place the organic matter in each jar. Then pour the rest of the soil into the jars.
5. Use a pushpin to puncture a few holes into the jar lids. The holes must be the same size, number, and location on each lid. Place the lids on the jars.
6. Observe the material each day.
7. When the material in one jar is decomposed, remove the organic material from the second jar and measure its mass.

Hints: The mass of the organic matter can be obtained daily but because the mold and odor will be unpleasant for many people this measurement should be done outside. As long as the jars are placed in the same area, the variables of outside temperature, air flow, and light are controlled. It would also be wise to take the temperature of each jar daily as the decomposition occurs.

TAKING IT FURTHER

What impact does food with a high sugar content have on a compost pile? If soil microbes are important in decomposition and they metabolize sugar similar to the way humans do, will they have a period of rapid decomposition (as noted by a rapid temperature increase) as they experience a sugar high?

How does water impact decomposition? Water is necessary for decomposition. This can be easily demonstrated by placing equal amounts of compost with soil in two jars and leaving the soil of one jar completely dry. Little decomposition will occur in the dry jar. For an even more dramatic effect, use dried fruit as the organic material. If some water is good, there is probably an upper limit so that more is not necessarily better. If too much water is added to a compost pile, it may kill the microbes as well as prevent air from getting to the mix.

How much air, if any, is necessary for decomposition? Put dirt and organic matter into two jars. Put the lid tightly on one jar and leave the lid off the experimental group. Some people use chicken wire or other wire mesh to increase airflow in their compost bins. Determine a way to increase passive airflow in your system.

Will mixing increase the rate of decomposition? If air is necessary for decomposition, then allowing more air to reach the mixture would be a good thing. Put dirt and organic matter into two separate jars. Shake one jar to mix daily and do not shake the control jar. The results might suggest that a composter should mix his or her pile by stirring it often.

How does the pH of the mixture impact decomposition? Adding lime to a compost pile to decrease the pH is sometimes suggested. Add substances that alter the pH of the compost and see what impact that has on the decomposition rate.

If the soil microorganisms are necessary for decomposition, is there an optimum pH at which they can reproduce most effectively? To adequately explore this question, a means of counting microorganism populations would need to be devised.

Would inoculating a new compost pile with older compost increase the rate of decay? Set up two jars with organic matter and soil. Add compost that has already partially decayed to one jar.

Does the species of worm used in a compost pile increase the rate of decay? Red worms (Eisenia fetida) are sometimes marketed for their compost creating potential. Compare the ability of two different species of worms to break down compost.

Does particle size affect the rate of decomposition? Make a compost pile out of materials that you shred in a food processor. In the control jar, leave the materials in large pieces.

Where Is North?

Earth & Space Science

BACKGROUND

The Earth spins on an imaginary axis that goes through the geographic North Pole. A compass points to the Earth's magnetic north pole and the direction the compass points depends on your location on the Earth's surface. The geographic North Pole is about 2,000 kilometers away from the magnetic north pole.

Interestingly, the Earth's magnetic poles have not always been where they are today. The poles have reversed many times and the cause of that reversal is not well understood. However, the direction of the magnetic poles can be found in igneous rocks that contain magnetic minerals.

QUESTION

How is the location of the North Pole different from the magnetic north pole?

RESEARCH TOPICS

magnetic north pole, geographic North Pole, directional compass, magnetism, magnetic pole

HYPOTHESIS

The Earth's magnetic north pole and geographical North Pole can be calculated if the angular difference between the two points is known.

MATERIALS

Compass, star map, hiking map with magnetic declination, pencil, blank paper, ruler, protractor

PROCEDURE

1. Go outside at night with the compass and star map. Use the map to find Polaris. Polaris is the North Star and can be found directly above the geographic North Pole also called true north. Since Polaris is directly above the Earth's rotational axis, it is always visible in the northern hemisphere night sky.
2. Make a line on the center of the paper. Line the straight line up with the geographic North Pole.
3. Use the directional compass to find the magnetic north pole. Mark the magnetic north on your paper.
4. Use the protractor to measure the degrees difference between the geographic North Pole and magnetic north pole.
5. Check other areas and determine the degrees difference between the geographic North Pole and magnetic north pole.

Data:

Location	Degrees Difference Between the Geographic and Magnetic North Poles
1 _____	
2 _____	
3 _____	

Hints: In some areas, the difference between the geographic North Pole and magnetic north poles is so slight that it can be ignored completely.

TAKING IT FURTHER

How can you demonstrate the presence of a magnetic field? Place a bar magnet horizontally on a table, then set several small compasses equidistantly around the bar magnet. This will show the direction of the magnetic field around the compass. The Earth's magnetic minerals have lined up in rocks the same way to show the magnetic field of the Earth.

What changes occur in the magnetic field of a magnet if the magnet has been weakened or strengthened? Before you plan your investigation, experiment to find the best way to observe a magnetic field. One technique to consider is to place the magnet beneath a piece of paper and sprinkle iron filings on the paper. For example, try turning the magnet the other way and see how different the picture becomes. Put two bar magnets horizontally beneath the paper so that their north poles are about 2 cm apart and sprinkle the iron filings on the paper. Repeat the same procedure but place the bar magnets so that the north pole of one is 2 cm from the south pole of the other bar magnet. The "picture" of the magnetic field can be preserved using a pump spray glue or other adhesive. These pictures can be slipped into plastic pockets and collated into your formal science journal.

Name _____   **Date** _____

Sizing Up the Sun and Moon

BACKGROUND

Though the moon is 386,000 kilometers away, it is our nearest neighbor of any appreciable size. In the distant past, the only way to study the moon was through a telescope. In 1959, the first spacecraft flew by the moon and collected information about the lunar surface. The moon has a diameter of about 3,479 kilometers but how can we verify that number from Earth?

QUESTION

Why does the moon appear larger than the sun when viewed from Earth?

RESEARCH TOPICS

Earth's moon, phases of the moon, perigee, apogee

HYPOTHESIS

If the distance from the Earth of a object in space is known, then the diameter of the object can be calculated.

MATERIALS

Meterstick, craft stick, calculator

PROCEDURE

1. Place the meterstick on a sturdy place such as a tree branch or fence so that you will be able to hold it steady.
2. Carefully adjust your position and that of the meterstick until the bottom of the moon appears to be touching the top of the meterstick. Your eye should be close to the zero end of the meterstick.
3. Hold the meterstick steady with one hand. Using the other hand, place the craft stick alongside the meterstick. Either hold the craft stick vertically or horizontally to match the diameter of the moon. Slide the craft stick alongside the meterstick until the width of the stick appears to cover the moon completely.
4. Determine the distance from the craft stick to your eye by reading the measurement on the meterstick.
5. Repeat steps 1–4 several times and record your measurements, then average the results.

Data:

Use the equation below:

$$\frac{\text{Moon diameter}}{\text{Earth to moon distance (386,000 km)}} = \frac{\text{width of craft stick (usually 1 cm)}}{\text{distance between the craft stick and your eye (cm)}}$$

The diameter of the moon is what you are trying to find so:

$$\text{Moon diameter} = \frac{\text{width of craft stick x 386,000 km}}{\text{distance between the stick and your eye}}$$

Hints: For obvious reasons, this experiment can only be done on the night of a full moon. The exact distance from the Earth to the moon at the time of measurement should be determined to get the most accurate moon diameter.

TAKING IT FURTHER

Why do the sun and the moon look like they are about the same size? The sun is much farther away than the moon so it appears smaller. No one should ever look at the sun directly because that can cause severe damage to the eye but science suppliers sell glasses and special filters that can be worn to observe the sun so scientists can make similar measurements.

How does the apparent diameter of the moon change as it moves through its phases? Repeat this procedure throughout the lunar cycle to collect data.

Locate other objects in the sky such as distant stars and see if you can calculate the diameter using different materials.

Name _____ **Date** _____

Gauging Greenhouse Gases

Earth & Space Science

BACKGROUND

The burning of fossil fuels to obtain energy to meet the needs of a burgeoning human population creates undesirable chemical by-products that are dangerous in the atmosphere. One of the chemical by-products that concerns some scientists is carbon dioxide. They think that the increase in carbon dioxide caused by the burning of fossil fuels is a major greenhouse gas, which absorbs solar energy and traps excess heat in the atmosphere. Within this century, carbon dioxide levels have risen alarmingly and so, too, have the worldwide temperatures. A continuation of the trend will likely have catastrophic consequences.

QUESTION

How does carbon dioxide in the Earth's atmosphere affect the air temperature?

RESEARCH TOPICS

Greenhouse effect, global warming, fossil fuel combustion

HYPOTHESIS

If the atmosphere has elevated levels of carbon dioxide, the temperature will increase.

MATERIALS

Two aquarium thermometers, tape, two clear plastic shoe boxes with lids, water, Alka-seltzer®*, two identical lamps with 200-watt bulbs.

PROCEDURE

1. Place the aquarium thermometers 3 cm below the opening of the shoe boxes so that they can be read from the outside of the box. Tape the thermometers in place.
2. Add water to each shoe box to a depth of 4 cm. Place the lid on each box.
3. Lift the lid of one box slightly and quickly drop in two Alka-seltzer tablets. The tablets will react with the water to produce carbon dioxide gas. Close the lid quickly to trap the carbon dioxide gas within the "atmosphere" of the box. Label the box.
4. Place one lamp above each box. The distance and location of the lamp above each box should be identical.
5. Take a temperature reading every ten minutes until three consecutive numbers read the same in each box.

*Alka-seltzer® is a registered trademark of Bayer Corporation.

Data:

Time (minutes)	Air Temperature Control	Variable
Start		
10		
20		
30		
40		

Time (minutes)	Air Temperature Control	Variable
50		
60		
70		
80		
90		

Hints: The water in each box represents the Earth's surface. To make a more accurate representation, cover one fourth of the box bottom with rocks, soil, and plants.

TAKING IT FURTHER

The boxes could be set up with soil and plants in various locations to make a more attractive display and a more realistic model of the planet.

How do plants react to higher levels of carbon dioxide and higher air temperatures? Many living things have only a very narrow temperature range that can be tolerated. Locate plant species, both aquatic and terrestrial, that may suffer in the box with the higher temperature and greater carbon dioxide concentration to investigate this problem.

There are two opposing views concerning global warming: one is that the warming is part of the Earth's natural cycle and the other is that human activities are increasing global temperatures. Either way, no one can claim that drastically increasing carbon dioxide levels through human activities will be good for the planet.

APPENDIX

Questions to Jump-start Your Search for a Topic

- Does the sense of sight affect the sense of taste?
- Are human mouths cleaner or dirtier than the mouths of dogs or cats?
- If you blindfold volunteers, do you slow down their reaction time?
- How does the size of a container affect how fast water evaporates?
- How different is the temperature in different parts of the same room?
- To what extent does a ceiling fan equalize the temperature in a room?
- What impact does wind have on cooling?
- How is erosion affected by ground cover?
- Do plants lose water through their leaves?
- How could you find out if tropical plants and desert plants lose different amounts of water (have different transpiration rates)?
- How does an increase in temperature impact how quickly materials dissolve?
- Does particle size affect the rate at which a substance dissolves?
- What factor has the greatest effect on the speed at which a seed will germinate?
- Why does the sun look so much larger when it is on the horizon at sunrise and sunset?
- How can the speed at which plants grow be increased?
- How can the speed a car travels down a ramp be increased?
- Can the roof color of a house affect the inside temperature of the house?
- What will help cut flowers stay fresh looking longer?
- How can you find out if the vitamins humans use are good for plants?
- What freezes faster, hot water or cold water?
- Does a watched pot ever boil?
- Why are rocks different colors?
- In what ways can you find out if different types of music increase a person's ability to concentrate?
- Why is the sky blue?
- Does the same substance that makes grass green also make leaves green?
- How do clouds form and make rain? What factors increase the amount of precipitation?
- What makes a rainbow?
- What makes meat turn colors?
- Does an apple a day really keep the doctor away?

- Does the same substance make all natural foods red?
- Why do oranges have seeds?
- Why does sugar disappear when you put it in water?
- Why are canned beets purple and beets at the salad bar red?
- How can metal ships float on water?
- Why can't you see stars during the day?
- Why does the ground get really hard and crack in some places when it is dry?
- What is the best way to prevent ice from forming on the windshield of a car or on the pavement?
- What is the best way to remove ice from a car's windshield once it has formed?
- How can snow be melted on a driveway without shoveling?
- Why is it hotter at the equator than the North Pole?
- How do you steer a sailboat?
- Why do your veins look blue but you bleed red?
- How does a television work?
- What makes holes in bread?
- How much faster is a cat's resting heart rate compared to a human's? A dog's resting heart rate?
- How are cartoons made?
- Do bright colors help us remember things better?
- What type of nut has the most energy?
- Can people really taste the difference between tap water and bottled water?
- What type of roof would hold up best during a hailstorm?
- Why do some hailstones get so big?
- What is the impact of mulch on weed control between crop rows?
- How do insect repellants affect plants?
- Do vegetables grow best in raised beds or in fields?
- Which type of breath mint leaves your mouth feeling cooler?
- What impact do oil spills have on the plants that grow in soil?
- Does fireplace ash make a good plant fertilizer?
- How can the strength of recycled paper be improved?
- What substances make effective, less toxic cleaning fluids?
- Why do you need thumbs?
- Which gum forms larger bubbles—gum with sugar or sugar-free gum?
- Since sugarless bubble gum is sold in smaller packages, do you get less gum?
- Do children of smokers have less athletic ability or reduced lung capacity?
- Do children of smokers get more illnesses?
- Is there a correlation between athletic ability and grades in school?
- Do children who play instruments do better in science and math classes?

The Most Common Properties Measured, Equipment, Unit, and Abbreviation

Property	Equipment Used	Unit	Abbreviation
Acidity/Alkalinity	pH meter or pH paper	pH	
Area	meterstick or metric ruler	square meter	m^2
		square centimeter	cm^2
		square millimeter	mm^2
Density	balance & meterstick	grams/cubic centimeter	g/cm^3
	balance & metric ruler	grams/cubic meter	g/cm^3
	balance & graduated cylinder	grams/milliliter	g/mL
Electrical			
Potential	voltmeter	volt	V
Current	ammeter	ampere	amp (A)
Resistance	ohmmeter	ohm	Ω
Force	spring scale	newton	N
Length, Width, or Height	meterstick or metric ruler	meter	m
		centimeter	cm
		millimeter	mm
Mass	balance	gram	g
		kilogram	kg
Speed	metric ruler and clock	meters/second	m/s
Temperature	thermometer	degrees Celsius	°C
Time	clock or stopwatch	seconds	s
Volume	beaker, graduated cylinder	milliliter	mL
		liter	L
	meterstick or metric ruler	cubic meter	m^3
		cubic centimeter	cm^3
Weight	spring scale	newton	N

Science Equipment Suppliers

Caroline Biological Supply Company
P.O. Box 6010
Burlington, NC 27216-6010
1-800-334-5551
Web site: www.carolina.com

Flinn Scientific, Inc.
P.O. Box 219
Batavia, IL 60510-0219
1-800-452-1261
Web site: www.flinnsci.com

Frey Science Company, Inc.
P.O. Box 8101

Mansfield, OH 44901
1-800-225-3739
Web site: www.freyscientific.com

Sargent-Welch
P.O. Box 529
Buffalo Grove, IL 60089
1-800-727-4368
Web site: www.sargentwelch.com

Sigma Chemical Company
P.O. Box 14508
St. Louis, MO 63178-9916
1-800-325-3010

Science Kit & Boreal Laboratories
777 East Park Drive
Tonawanda, NY 14150-6784
1-800-828-7777
Web site: www.sciencekit.com

Wards Natural Science Establishment, Inc.
P.O. Box 92912
Rochester, NY 14692-9012
1-800-962-2660
Web site: wardsci.com